and

tion

Issues for
Counsellors

10/5 2pm

REFERENCE

PROFESSIONAL SKILLS FOR COUNSELLORS

The *Professional Skills for Counsellors* series, edited by Colin Feltham, covers the practical, technical and professional skills and knowledge which trainee and practising counsellors need to improve their competence in key areas of therapeutic practice.

Titles in the series include:

Medical and Psychiatric Issues for Counsellors
Brian Daines, Linda Gask and Tim Usherwood

Personal and Professional Development for Counsellors
Paul Wilkins

Counselling by Telephone
Maxine Rosenfield

Time-Limited Counselling
Colin Feltham

Client Assessment
Stephen Palmer and Gladeana McMahon (eds)

Counselling, Psychotherapy and the Law
Peter Jenkins

Referral and Termination Issues for Counsellors

Anne Leigh

SAGE Publications
London • Thousand Oaks • New Delhi

SAGE Publications Ltd
6 Bonhill Street
London EC2A 4PU

SAGE Publications Inc.
2455 Teller Road
Thousand Oaks, California 91320

SAGE Publications India Pvt Ltd
32, M-Block Market
Greater Kailash – I
New Delhi 110 048

British Library Cataloguing in Publication data

A catalogue record for this book is available
from the British Library

ISBN 0 8039 7474 4
ISBN 0 8039 7475 2 (pbk)

Library of Congress catalog card number 98–060212

Typeset by Mayhew Typesetting, Rhayader, Powys
Printed in Great Britain by Biddles Ltd, Guildford, Surrey

To Jon, Dan, Jen, Dan and Kira with love

Contents

Acknowledgements

My grateful thanks go to all those who have allowed me to use their stories, poems and experiences and who completed the survey. Thank you to Colin for his constant help and patience. Thank you to my family, to whom this book is dedicated, and my special friends, Jill, Mike, Paul and Sheila. My thanks also go to Marian who painstakingly checked all the resource details.

1

Introduction: Why Referral and Termination Issues are Crucial

There are many important and fascinating issues raised for the counsellor when contemplating aspects of referral and termination of clients in counselling. There are the decisions that have to be made about the appropriateness of referral of a client to an alternative avenue of therapy or help, how to handle referrals from other practitioners, and how to deal with the process of termination of counselling. There may be powerful feelings for both client and counsellor which we need to be able to handle in a caring and professional way.

The skills concerned with referring a client and terminating with a client have similarities in that both situations need to be conducted with skill and due sensitivity to the needs of both client and counsellor. A referral of a client to another practitioner usually signifies an ending of the work between the client and counsellor whether it be after the first interview or after many sessions, and so a referral can be seen as an aspect of termination. When receiving a referral from another practitioner we may possibly have to deal with unfinished business to do with endings between the client and the previous therapist. An important difference between referral and termination procedures in counselling is that referral of a client means that the counselling work needs to continue, albeit with another counsellor or professional, whereas termination with a client may mean that the client has finished counselling altogether. With some knowledge and preparation, both situations can be handled in a way that maximizes gains and minimizes losses, both for the client and the counsellor.

It is important for the counsellor to ensure that she is aware of the expertise offered in the local vicinity, and further afield, in the form of other therapists, community mental health teams and self-help groups, for example. However much we, as counsellors, would like to be 'all things to all people' the reality is that sometimes an onward referral is very much in the interests of the client, and occasionally is essential for the counsellor involved. Sometimes a counsellor responds to a client's needs inappropriately, wanting to help but not having the necessary expertise and so becoming embroiled in a difficult situation which may be detrimental for both parties. The recognition of this could be an impetus for professional development for the future. Referrals need to be handled with careful regard to the feelings of the client, who may believe that his problem is too much for even his counsellor to handle unless the situation is carefully explained and choices presented. It may not be easy for the counsellor to tell a client that someone else may be able to offer a better service for the client's needs, but it is essential that we know and accept our limitations in the areas where we cannot help, and that we are aware of other professionals who can offer specialist help. We need to have the relevant information readily available so that we can make an effective referral. The hard work that is necessary to keep our referral information up to date will not only benefit our clients but will also give us contact with other professionals and a chance to advertise our own areas of expertise.

Some practitioners of particular therapeutic orientations may not believe in the necessity of referral. Carl Rogers believed that anything that was accepted by a client because it was taught by another person was of no use and that the most that could be accomplished was a temporary change, which would soon disappear, 'leaving the individual more than ever convinced of his inadequacy' (Rogers, 1989: 33). Rogers believed that lasting change and growth could result only from the client's finding a healing capacity within himself as a result of experiencing a certain type of therapeutic relationship. This relationship established by the counsellor would show the core conditions of unconditional positive regard, empathic communication of understanding, and congruence.

Although the relationship between the client and counsellor is usually of the utmost importance, it may not be potent enough for some client difficulties. Sometimes expertise in a certain area, such as behavioural desensitization for phobic conditions, for example, is necessary for some clients. It could be argued that no one counselling orientation is sufficient for all client problems and no one counsellor can hope to be exactly right for all clients.

The first time onward referral may be considered by the counsellor is during the initial contact, which may be when the client makes an enquiry about counselling or when the first interview takes place. If the client states his problem over the telephone the counsellor may know at this early stage whether or not she might be able to offer counselling to this person and may be able to give some information to the client about alternative forms of help if necessary. If the client has been offered an appointment by a letter written by an intermediary, the first time the client communicates with the counsellor may be at the initial interview and the counsellor will be assessing whether or not she and the client can form a working relationship. It may be then that the counsellor identifies that other areas of expertise are required.

The counsellor may, for instance, refer the client for a medical opinion if the counsellor suspects that there is a significant physical rather than, or as well as, a psychological problem (Daines et al., 1997). If the client is showing highly aggressive impulses towards himself or others or is displaying signs of mental illness, a psychiatric referral may be indicated. Some clients may present with problems that may benefit from a different clinical or theoretical orientation or other forms of counselling such as group therapy, family or couple therapy (Palmer and McMahon, 1997). Sometimes the client may indicate at the first interview that he would prefer a counsellor of a particular gender, race, religion or sexual orientation and it may be possible to accommodate his wishes if the counsellor knows of anyone suitable, or works in a team providing counsellors from various backgrounds. There may be indications that the client needs focused work as in time-limited counselling or more long-term work that may not be available in the particular setting in which the counsellor is working.

Once counsellor and client have established a working relationship there may still be other times when referral is indicated.

Often a client will present with one problem but there may be other issues underneath, and upon reflection the counsellor may feel that the client might benefit from seeing another professional or using another resource. For instance, the client may seem to have problems with alcohol or drug addiction and may have been advised to see a counsellor specializing in this area, but on further investigation it is revealed that the fundamental problem is that of childhood sexual abuse. The counsellor specializing in drug or alcohol addiction may or may not have the expertise or confidence to deal with sexual abuse. Upon discussion with the client, the idea of referral to another professional may be acceptable to both client and counsellor and the referral made easily. However, sometimes the counsellor may think that she can, or feel that she should be able to, cope with the issue that has arisen, or the client may be resistant to the idea of referral. This is a situation that needs to be discussed with the counsellor's supervisor and carefully monitored as there may be transference or counter-transference issues involved. A referral in what might be expected to be the middle phase of counselling is probably a forced ending and needs to be handled sensitively as there could be a variety of feelings, such as regret, sadness or frustration, for both counsellor and client. There are sometimes unfortunate instances when both counsellor and client would wish to continue but one of them moves house or changes job, and here again this premature termination needs to be handled sensitively.

When the ending of counselling approaches, there are various considerations to take into account. Often the ending occurs naturally when both counsellor and client review the progress that has been made and both feel ready to terminate counselling. However, sometimes there can be an abrupt ending by the client which can leave the counsellor in a quandary as to what happened to cause this and what to do about it, or there may be reluctance on either the client's or counsellor's side to terminate counselling. In both cases there may be one particular feeling or a mixture of feelings, such as concern, anxiety, regret, sadness, annoyance, anger, frustration, guilt, a sense of surprise, puzzlement or confusion, dissatisfaction, disappointment, inadequacy, failure or rejection, and even sometimes a feeling of relief or pleasure. In answer to a question in a questionnaire given to practising counsellors and trainee counsellors (Appendix 1, Question 16), many counsellors identified the sensation of being 'left hanging' or 'unfinished'. Sometimes supervision or personal counselling is needed to clarify what happened between client and counsellor and whether some of the counsellor's own issues have been triggered.

Of course practitioners from different orientations have different views on the importance of termination. Some counsellors, particularly of the cognitive-behavioural orientation, may sometimes negotiate, say, six or ten sessions of counselling with the client and be content to terminate counselling after having a review of the client's progress in the last session. At the other extreme a psychodynamic counsellor or psychotherapist may stipulate several weeks or even months of termination work in order to thoroughly explore all the feelings and meanings that may arise for the client.

There is also the style of termination to consider. Some counsellors may offer a set number of sessions through choice or because they are working for an agency that only offers a certain number of sessions, and then the counselling has to finish. Other counsellors may be more flexible and offer a staggered approach to termination which may take the form of fortnightly sessions, followed by monthly sessions for a while. Some counsellors may offer a follow-up session. Sometimes a counsellor may tell the client that he may contact her in the future if he needs to at any time.

Endings can be seen to be traumatic and best avoided or postponed, or satisfactory and even joyful. Unfortunately, many people have had traumatic experiences of endings and have, as a result, developed an intense fear of ending relationships. Through personal communications it appears that some counsellors may themselves have difficulties with endings and so may be less able to deal with their clients' feelings about termination of counselling. Later in the book there will be an exploration of difficult endings for either client or counsellor. There is also a look at ways to make the termination of counselling a creative and satisfying experience.

There is a chapter on the importance of being aware of some of the ethical considerations in referral and termination issues. The British Association for Counselling's Code of Ethics and Practice for Counsellors stipulates that counsellors must be aware of their competence levels and work within their limitations of competence (BAC, 1996a: A.4., B.2.2.17, B.2.2.19). This means that counsellors need to attend to their professional needs in order to give appropriate counselling for each client and be aware of the advisability of referral to other professionals if necessary for the client's well-being. Counsellors need to examine their personal financial needs, and be able to balance their need for adequate remuneration with aspects such as the fatigue factor if working for an agency, or a possible tendency to hang on to clients if working privately. Also, is it ever ethical to accept payment for making referrals as reportedly happens in some US settings (Stout, 1993)? Counsellors need to be vigilant about fulfilling their own emotional needs outside their counselling work. There is a strong case for the expectation of responsible care by the counsellor for her client which would begin at the time she is approached by a prospective client and continue until the counselling contract is terminated or a referral is satisfactorily achieved. Some practitioners would argue that this expectation of caring might extend even beyond this last session in the form of availability to the client. And to take matters even further, it has been suggested that the counsellor should make arrangements for the future care of his or her clients in the event of the counsellor's death (Trayner and Clarkson, 1992).

It is important for our clients' benefit and our peace of mind to keep our personal resource directory up to date. We should ideally have a list of both national and local resources available and make every effort to enquire frequently at local health centres and help agencies as to what is being offered in the form of therapy and self-help groups. The questionnaire (Appendix 1, Question 9) showed that approximately two-thirds of the counsellors who answered that question indicated that they kept an up-to-date file of professionals' details for referral purposes. Some counselling courses now stipulate that students make such a resource directory as part of their coursework assignments. Some areas of the country have a local counselling network which could make for easier personal knowledge of particular expertise. If there is no local network it may be that you wish to visit or telephone potential referral contacts.

In this book I will explore some of the issues, both emotional and practical, that may arise for both counsellors and clients in the referral and termination processes. A short questionnaire has been given to some practising counsellors and trainee counsellors in order to determine what counsellors are actually doing in their practices (Appendix 1). I have asked counselling colleagues for their experiences and I have used examples of counsellor and client interactions which are essentially genuine but sometimes presented as composites of similar kinds of experiences. All names have been changed and any identifying details altered. To quote M. Scott Peck (1990) 'If you think you recognise one of my specific patients in this book, you will be wrong'. It is possible that sometimes there is no definitive answer to a particular dilemma, but an investigation into possible alternatives and outcomes by sharing experiences may assist counsellors in reflecting upon their professional careers.

It has been interesting to discover that, although referral is an important issue for counsellors, there is little reference to the topic in the therapeutic literature. I found a journal article written in 1962 which states that 'referral is an old, recognized, and frequently used aspect of counselling, but a survey of the literature shows that it is a much neglected topic' (Ramsey, 1962). Another article about referral of clients, written in 1991, states that 'surprisingly little has been written on the topic' (Halgin and Caron, 1991). The situation is similar a few years later in that it is difficult to find much written about referring clients. The topic is mentioned relatively briefly in various books on general counselling issues, and there is a short recent publication by PCCS Books in their Incomplete Guide series (Williams, 1993). It is interesting to speculate why there seems to be an avoidance of this most important area. It may be that some counsellors do not realize how essential it is to think about the possibility of referring clients. I remember how concerned I felt when I was talking to an extremely experienced counsellor about referrals and he said that he never referred clients because there was no-one to refer to. I have also noted that many enthusiastic newly qualified counsellors tend to believe that they can deal with everyone and everything and, unfortunately, their inexperience may lead them to fail to recognize client problems that are beyond their competence levels. This is when an experienced supervisor is needed to guide the inexperienced counsellor. I hope that this book goes some way towards exploring some of the issues, decisions and feelings involved for both counsellors and clients when dealing with referrals.

The literature on termination issues in counselling is, however, plentiful. Many therapists of different persuasions have attempted

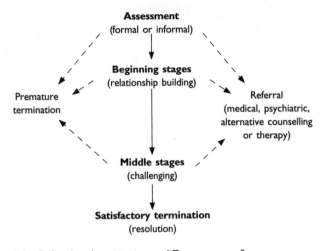

Figure 1.1   *Referral and termination at different stages of counselling*

to tackle some of the difficulties involved with endings and have come to their own conclusions. The psychoanalytic literature in particular explores in depth the feelings of the client when contemplating termination of therapy, and some authors have also approached the aspects that affect the therapist (Kupers, 1988; Siebold, 1991).

Lastly, I will declare my own personal interest in this exploration of referral and termination issues. My first counselling experience was initiated because the training I was undertaking strongly recommended that students engage in their own counselling. This experience ended disastrously for me when my counsellor decided that I needed to see someone else because she identified too strongly with my issues and she ended the counselling abruptly. It took me six months to find a counsellor whom I could trust and then six further months of counselling before I began to feel less pain and devastation. I do not wish anyone to undergo such unnecessary suffering. Unfortunately, literature on the client's experience of counselling shows that bad or unsatisfactory experiences are not at all uncommon (Masson, 1990; Sutherland, 1987). As professional counsellors working to a code of ethics, we have a duty to our clients and ourselves to be aware of our limitations as counsellors and to be able to handle referrals to other practitioners and termination of counselling with sensitivity and responsibility (BAC, 1996a: 2.2.17).

Summary of referrals and termination at different stages of counselling

Referrals and termination at different stages of counselling are summarized below and in Figure 1.1.

■ *Beginning stage*: Assessment may indicate referral for specific help (for instance, medical or psychiatric intervention, different counselling orientation or alternative counselling arenas).
■ *Middle stage*: Referral is due to geographical factors, short-term to long-term counselling or irreconcilable differences between counsellor and client.
■ *Ending stage*: Termination takes place of this particular form of counselling, but there is the possibility of referral to a different kind of counselling at a later time.

2

The Beginning Phase

This chapter explores the initial stages of the counselling contract, from the first contact with the client, receiving referrals, initial assessment and the discussion of termination with the client if this is appropriate. From the very first contact with the client the counsellor is assessing whether or not counselling is the best option and, if referral is indicated, to whom the client should be directed.

The first contact

Whether you are receiving a referral or the client is self-referring, the first contact between you and your client is likely to be in the form of either a letter or a telephone conversation. Occasionally, a new client may present as an emergency or a 'drop-in' service is offered, and the first contact will then be face-to-face. This may well be a crisis intervention but, as well as dealing with the presenting problem, arrangements can be made for further counselling appointments.

If you are working in a GP's surgery or for an agency such as an alcohol counselling service, the usual procedure is for clients to be referred to you by letter and then an appointment will be sent by you to the client. Sometimes this letter may be sent routinely by an intermediary. As this letter is the first communication by you to your potential client it is important that as well as containing all the information that the client requires, such as time and place of appointment and also a telephone number in case the appointment is not suitable, you also appear to be friendly and approachable, as the whole idea of counselling or therapy can be frightening for a new client. A client may have many anxieties about going to see a counsellor, but 'a common element throughout, however, is vulnerability' (Dryden and Feltham, 1992). Some studies have been carried out to determine the most common client fears, such as 'friends thinking I'm abnormal for coming' or 'counselor thinking I'm a bad person', in order to develop an instrument to measure client fears (Pipes et al., 1985).

If you are working in a private setting or employee counselling or student counselling, a potential client will probably contact you by phone, or you will be phoning the client. It is important for you to decide how much information you will give to the client on the phone and whether you wish to know something about the reason for his coming to see you. The client may desire to know some details of your qualifications and theoretical orientation and whether you are able to work with his particular problem. One of the difficulties that may arise for the unwary counsellor is to enter into a prolonged counselling session on the phone, and it can be galling after half an hour to have the potential client say that he feels so much better that he does not need to come and see you! On the other hand the client may well just state that he will 'think about it'. Sometimes an intermediary will make the appointment for you by phone, and in this case it is important to monitor the client's response to this because the personal contact with you may be important. This may mean your asking the client how he responded or, if he did not appear, trying to establish that personal contact yourself through letter or phone.

Key practice point

The client's first contact with the counsellor will be either by receiving a letter or telephone call offering an appointment, or by face-to-face contact if there is a 'drop-in' service or crisis service, so you need to be appropriately prepared and monitor how the client experiences this first communication.

Non-attendance

Sometimes, of course, the client does not arrive for the first appointment. There may be many reasons for a non-attendance but one of these could be fear. If a person has never been to a counsellor before, there may be some apprehension and possibly some feeling of shame because he 'should be able to cope'. There may be confusion in the client's mind about the role of the counsellor and whether or not seeing a counsellor means that he is going crazy. Often the client may need reassurance about his reactions – for instance prolonged outbursts of crying 'for no particular reason' after bereavement, or extreme irritability during stress – because the client may never have experienced such a 'loss of control' before and that in itself is frightening. If the counsellor is seen to accept the client and his situation, give information about the counselling role and what counselling can offer, this will go a long way in establishing trust and laying the foundations of the working relationship between counsellor and client. In a GP surgery, although there may be some reassurance because it is a familiar place to the client, there may also be a reinforcement of the ideas of 'sickness' and 'cure'; also, if told by their doctor to try counselling, some clients may automatically believe that they are 'mind-sick' and so fear being thought mad.

Some counsellors decide to phone the client if he has not arrived within twenty minutes or so. This may prove to be bene-ficial because talking to the client on the phone is more personal than communication by letter, and it shows the client that the counsellor is concerned enough to bother to find out why he did not turn up for the appointment. Another appointment can be arranged, and often the client will arrive for this second appoint-ment. However, it is possible that the client would be embar-rassed by a phone call, and some clients do not wish their family to know that they are considering counselling.

If the client cannot be contacted by phone, or the counsellor prefers to communicate by letter, a follow-up letter can be sent offering another appointment. It is quite usual to offer this second chance for an appointment unless waiting lists are so long that this is impossible.

Key practice point

If the client does not attend the first appointment, it is usual to offer another appointment either by telephone or letter. Some clients may not wish to be phoned at home or work.

Receiving referrals from another professional

Sometimes referrals will be made to you by another counsellor or therapist. It may be that the therapist has no vacancies, or that you have an expertise in a certain area or that the other therapist is moving to another part of the country. Ideally, the other therapist will contact you first in order to ask you whether you are willing to accept this referral, and possibly she will give you some information about the client (with the client's permission). I had the unpleasant experience of receiving a referral letter from a counsellor about a client I had seen a few years previously and who wished to see me again. Unfortunately, I was no longer in a position to see this client, since at the time I was working only for specific GP surgeries. I then had to explain, on the phone, to this ex-client that I could not see her although she had been informed by her present counsellor that I would be able to. Although her initial reaction was one of distress, when the situation was explained to her the client was happy to stay with her present counsellor. This situation need never have arisen if the counsellor had contacted me first and asked me whether or not I was in a position to see this particular client. The only pleasant part about the whole incident was that I had news of this client who, in my opinion, had terminated prematurely, and in fact she was doing extremely well and was just looking for some more support in order to maintain her improvement.

If you receive a referral from another counsellor, psychologist or psychotherapist, it is important to spend as much time as is needed on the client's feelings about the referral. While it may appear to the practitioner involved to be the sensible option to refer this client, it may appear differently to the client. The client may feel rejected, or that his problem is so bad that no-one can deal with it, or there may be anger. If these feelings are not explored there may be resistance from the client in the new counselling situation. Of course it may be some time before these feelings are expressed by the client, because he may not feel safe enough to, for instance, express anger because he is afraid that he may be 'passed on' yet again.

> ***Example***   *A client who was referred to a counsellor did not express her anger until the sixth session. There came a point in this session when she became silent and the counsellor*

very quickly sensed that there seemed to be a problem that was not being expressed, so she asked the client if she was comfortable with the silence. This precipitated an outburst where it was evident that her last therapist had used silence a lot and the client had felt very threatened and frightened and then very angry with him and in fact had stormed out of the room. She was unable to articulate her anger, and it seemed as though the previous therapist had then himself felt threatened, because there appeared to be a history of the therapist's cancelling appointments and arriving late. After being able to talk about her past experiences with this therapist, this client was then able to talk about her sexual abuse as a child and was able to express her feelings of anger about that.

It may also be that you could receive a referral from a different kind of therapist, such as a complementary therapist. For example, there have been instances where certain body therapies such as aromatherapy, Alexander Technique and shiatsu have resulted in release of body memories which neither the client nor therapist has been able to deal with, and as a result, counselling is indicated. The client may be in crisis and need work at a deeper level than is usual at the beginning stages of counselling.

If you have received a referral from another practitioner, you may wish to contact that person in order to receive any relevant information about the client, with the client's permission. The other practitioner may also appreciate a letter from you about the progress of the client, again with the client's permission.

Key practice point

Allow the client to express any negative feelings about referral from another practitioner; this may happen later in the counselling process when the client feels safe.

Receiving referrals from inside an agency

If you are working as a counsellor within a multidisciplinary team you will most likely receive referrals from other members of that team. The head of the service will be aware of the expertise of the members of the team and be able to refer clients to the appropriate professional. If the team has regular meetings, each member will also become familiar with the different skills and abilities of each colleague so that cross-referral can take place if needed.

Sometimes it is necessary to be assertive about your counselling capabilites, as some heads of service may have rigid ideas about the kind of clients or problems that are suitable for counselling. For instance a mental health team may decide that counselling is only appropriate for short-term work and that any client needing longer-term therapy or deeper work needs to see a psychologist or psychotherapist. If you have experience with longer-term work and/or deeper therapeutic work you may need to make this clear to the head of the team, who may not realize what counselling can offer. If you are a newly qualified counsellor you may need to be assertive about the necessity for professional development either by further training or by being allowed to see more challenging clients while receiving adequate supervision.

Key practice point

Be assertive about your abilities and professional development when working for a multidisciplinary team.

Initial assessment by a senior counsellor

If you are working for an agency, such as an alcohol counselling service, or for a mental health team, it may be that all the clients are assessed by a senior counsellor before you see them. This may be an excellent practice if you are starting out as a counsellor, because you will be more likely to receive clients who are within your competence range and you will be able to build up your confidence and expertise. There is a tendency for the newly fledged enthusiastic counsellor to want to take on all comers and then painfully learn that there are some clients who are better served by either more experienced counsellors or some other kind of therapy altogether.

Although the initial assessment is performed by the senior counsellor, this does not necessarily mean that there will not be problems later on. Sometimes the presenting problem is only the tip of the iceberg, so the counsellor has always to be aware of the possibility of referral back to the senior counsellor or at least needs to ask for some consultation about the wisdom of continuing with the client.

> **Example**　*A client with whom I worked when I was training appeared to be suffering from mild depression and a general dissatisfaction with life. She received an initial assessment from a senior counsellor and was thought to be suitable for a trainee counsellor. After ten sessions she seemed much better and we discussed termination. About a month later she phoned up in great distress and was talking about suicide. After forty minutes on the phone she was feeling better, we fixed a time for an appointment and I was left feeling like a wrung-out dish cloth! It appeared that this client was in fact suffering from manic-depressive psychosis and had developed powerful superficial coping mechanisms that only broke down under extremely stressful conditions. Needless to say she needed much more intensive and specialist therapeutic help.*

There are drawbacks to the initial assessment's being performed by a senior counsellor. The first session can be a difficult one for both counsellor and client but it is a time when the client can begin to judge whether or not the counsellor can be trusted with his particular difficulty. If the first session is taken by one counsellor and then a second counsellor takes over, this can feel confusing for the client. It may be that the client has poured out the story of his life and has to repeat it for the second counsellor. A powerful rapport can be built in the first session, and the client may resent having to see another counsellor. Also it is sometimes the case that the client may be able to come to some resolution of his difficulties within one session. I have found this to be the case when the client has a specific problem and is allowed to explore this without the interference of a formal assessment procedure. Some research undertaken by Wise and Rinn (1983) showed that client drop-out rates could be significantly reduced if the clients were seen by the same person for assessment and subsequent therapy.

Key practice point

Client assessment by a senior counsellor can be useful for newly qualified counsellors who need to build confidence within their competence range. However, the first session is often the first step in building the trust between client and counsellor that is so important in the counselling relationship.

Initial assessment by you

Some kind of assessment, whether formal or not, is carried out in the first session in order to discover whether or not the counsellor and client can work together. It is at this point that the counsellor may suspect that a referral would possibly be more beneficial for the client.

Whether or not you perform a formal assessment procedure with every client depends on where you are working and your orientation. If you are working for a counselling agency or mental health team, you will have to follow whatever procedures are expected. If you are working in a private setting, it is your choice whether or not you formally assess your clients. If your orientation is person-centred, it is unlikely that you will be formally assessing your clients, whilst if your orientation is cognitive-behavioural, it is more likely that there will be a formal assessment.

Most counsellors in private practice probably do not use the first session for a formal assessment procedure (see Question 1 in Appendix 1). It is a time during which the counsellor is establishing whether or not she and the client can work together – whether the counsellor can offer what the client is looking for. The working relationship necessary between counsellor and client is something that needs to be negotiated on an individual basis. A formal assessment procedure may not be appropriate because of the nature of the questions asked by the counsellor, which may be seen by the client as intrusive or irrelevant at this time. An extensive series of questions by the counsellor may interfere with the formation of a trusting relationship. The client may feel that the counsellor is not listening to his concerns but is too intent upon receiving the correct answers to his questions. Unfortunately, a prolonged questioning session may reinforce the power imbalance where one person is totally in control of the session. Of course it may be that the client finds the questions comforting, as the counsellor is seen as 'taking over' the problem, and this may cause problems later on when the counsellor is trying to help the client find their own resources in order to deal with their difficulties.

The formal assessment procedure may cause conflict when the counsellor works for a multidisciplinary team. There appears to be a push towards formal assessments, notes kept in the office, and sharing of information within the team. It is understandable that a mental health team would wish information to be readily available if the counsellor wishes to refer the client or if there is an emergency, but there are implications for the practice of confidentiality. One of the positive aspects of the counselling contract is the assurance of confidentiality. The client may feel extremely concerned that no-one else is privy to his innermost feelings and thoughts and expects that the material discussed should remain contained within the counselling situation. In a private setting it is possible to reassure the client that everything that is discussed in counselling sessions is strictly confidential subject to the understanding that the counsellor is regularly seeing a supervisor, which is a requirement of membership of a professional body, for instance, the British Association for Counselling. I find that clients respond positively to the idea of counselling supervision if I talk about it being like 'a second opinion'. If the counsellor's notes are open to other professionals, this level of confidentiality is breached. Some counsellors will, in this situation, keep two sets of notes, so that in cases of emergency the necessary minimal information is available. However, the client has the right to see all health records, and the police may apply for a warrant which authorizes them to see all notes kept about the client (Jenkins, 1997).

This concept of confidentiality which is so important in the counselling situation may also be threatened by the possible necessity of breaching the confidentiality if the client is thinking of harming himself or others. Some counsellors will broach this subject in the first session and explain that confidentiality will be broken in these circumstances. To support a suicidal or aggressive client is a heavy burden that some counsellors would not wish to take on and so would decide to refer to another professional, usually a psychiatrist. However, some counsellors feel that if the client is told in the first session that the counsellor will have to break confidentiality if the client indicates suicidal intentions, then this may stop the client talking about any such thoughts that he is experiencing. Suicidal thoughts are common for clients under-going crises and can be useful if the client then discovers what he has to live for and can contact an inner strength in order to deal with the present situation. With such clients an acknowledgement of their depth of feeling combined with support and encourage-ment to find their own resources may be sufficient to help them through. Some clients, however, may feel so demoralized that they need extra help in the form of medication, and so the counsellor needs to be aware of the need to refer to the client's doctor or to a psychiatrist.

Some counsellors will have no problems with a formal assess-ment procedure, particularly if the counsellor is working in a cognitive-behavioural way. There is an example of a formal assessment outline in Appendix 3. Some counsellors are very comfortable working with what is essentially a medically oriented model, where a diagnosis is looked for and treatment prescribed. As Arnold Lazarus states, 'When real problems have been identi-fied, effective remedies can be administered' (Lazarus, 1989). In Lazarus's Multimodal Therapy the initial interview is seen as extremely important in order to assess the needs of each indi-vidual client. Some counsellors may send out a form for the clients to fill in and bring to the first interview. I have had the experience of working with clients who have been through this procedure, and they have frankly told me that they did not feel able to give the information asked for because they had not established a relationship with the counsellor and so felt that they would be too exposed if, for instance, they had written about their problems with sexuality or abuse.

Whatever orientation the counsellor has or wherever the counsellor is working, there are certain questions that he or she has in mind upon meeting a client for the first time. Funda-mentally, the counsellor is asking the question, 'Can we work together?' As we are all individuals with different expertise and experience, this question can only be answered by the particular counsellor and particular client in that special first session. For instance, one counsellor may not wish to work with a client presenting with an eating disorder and so will refer to another practitioner who is experienced in this field. The client may find it impossible to continue to see a counsellor of a particular gender, age, demeanour, or sexual orientation and so may ask to be referred to someone more suited. There may be indications at this initial interview that the particular problem with which the client is presenting, such as a phobia or bereavement, may indicate a particular therapeutic style such as directive or non-directive counselling. However, difficulties may arise if a counsellor believes that she can work with anyone who wishes to receive counselling or if the client is too distressed or unassertive to shop around.

There are other questions that the counsellor needs to keep in mind at the initial meeting. For instance, 'Is the client stable enough for counselling, and can counselling offer enough for this client?' Counselling is not a universal panacea; there are limitations in its usage and it may not always be the best choice for the client. If, for instance, the client is unable to communicate because of extreme withdrawal or incoherent thought patterns that leave the listener bewildered, there may be indications that the client is better suited to psychiatric intervention. For more detailed information on assessment of clients refer to Palmer and McMahon (1997).

Key practice points

1   You may wish, or you may be obliged, to use a formal assessment procedure with every client.
2   You need to determine whether or not the client is suitable for counselling or would be better served with a referral to an alternative practitioner.

Discussion of termination with the client at the beginning of counselling

Sometimes a client will ask the counsellor in the first session how many sessions are required. This is usually an impossible question to answer. Some clients may only need one session while others may need hundreds of sessions. However, it may be that you are restricted in the number of sessions that you can offer a client and so the notion of termination needs to be addressed in the first session.

Some counsellors work strictly to a limited number of sessions by choice or circumstances, and this must be made explicit to the client in, or before, the first session. Sometimes the number of sessions is limited by choice of the counsellor because this is the preferred way of working. More often the counsellor is working for an agency, employee assistance programme (EAP), or GP surgery where the number of sessions that can be offered is prescribed. The clear anticipation of termination focuses the work for both counsellor and client. There is some evidence to show that much progress can be made in the first three sessions, and some counsellors will see a client for two sessions and then offer a follow-up session (Barkham, 1989). Howard et al. (1986) showed in their research that measurable improvement could be demonstrated in forty-one per cent of clients after four sessions. Other counsellors may offer six sessions with a review in the sixth session, or perhaps twelve sessions with a review half way through and then termination at the twelfth session. Some clients work extremely well with such a system, and both counsellor and client may find it secure and productive.

Summary

1 Your first contact with a client, whether by phone or by letter, needs to be handled so that the client receives the necessary information in an efficient but approachable fashion.

2 A second appointment offered for a 'non-attender' will sometimes result in the client's attending.

3 If a client is referred to you by another counsellor, time should be given to any thoughts or feelings with which the client is left.

4 An initial assessment made by a senior counsellor is often useful for newly qualified counsellors.

5 Some counsellors use a formal assessment procedure and other counsellors do not. However, all counsellors look for information about the suitability of counselling for each individual client.

6 Discussion of termination, or expectations about the length, of counselling in the beginning stage may help to focus the counselling work.

3

Medical Referrals

During the first counselling session especially, but also throughout the whole counselling contract, we need to be alert to the possibility of the advisability of referring to a medical expert. Extreme forms of behaviour such as suicide attempts, violence and psychotic episodes indicate the need for psychiatric assessment. Some forms of fatigue, emotional lability, anxiety and depressive states may all result from a physiological or hormonal imbalance that could be helped by investigations and treatment from a medical practitioner. Some clients could benefit from a specialist approach such as behavioural desensitization for phobias, or a group dealing with anxiety or assertiveness, which could be available from the Community Mental Health Team contactable through the client's general practitioner. Also it is helpful to be aware of the complementary therapies available that could be used in conjunction with counselling.

Referral for psychiatric assessment

The bottom line is 'Can counselling help this client?' Warning signs may be where there is a history of suicidal or extreme aggressive impulses, serious alcohol abuse, obsessive compulsive disorder, personality disorder, severe depression or psychosis. It may be that you have a special training, ability or experience in dealing with these kinds of problems, but it is always useful to have a second opinion and back-up. There are also some people who need psychotropic drugs and other forms of psychiatric intervention in order to control their problematic thoughts, feelings or behaviour.

Example   *A client was referred to a counsellor from a psychiatrist, because the client specifically wanted to explore his feelings about his over-protected childhood. Upon reading his medical notes it appeared that as well as suffering from epilepsy from childhood, this client had been diagnosed both manic-depressive and paranoid schizophrenic and was taking a cocktail of anti-psychotic drugs. However, the client appeared to be stable and was able to explore his feelings about his parents and his sheltered childhood. When he indicated that he would like to stop taking all the drugs he was prescribed, he was promptly referred back to his psychiatrist as being the most suitable person to determine whether or not the client's wish was possible.*

Suicidal clients

It is sometimes the case that a client will indicate suicidal thoughts. It is important to explore such thoughts in order to ascertain whether or not there is any serious intent. Are there any specific plans for suicide? How strong are the feelings? Can the client cope with these thoughts and feelings? There may be a need for an emergency psychiatric admission.

Example   *A client was referred to a psychiatrist because the client could not cope with her suicidal feelings. She would have thoughts of suicide on her mind all the time and had planned a particular way of killing herself. She had tried this once before and had 'chickened out'. Even the thought of her family did not stop her, as she thought that they would be better off without her. She could not make any sort of contract about not killing herself. She hated herself and saw no point in living. The counsellor felt that he needed the reassurance of her doctor's back-up and also the opinion of a psychiatrist. The client was prescribed a powerful anti-depressant which helped to contain the suicidal urges and then she bravely undertook a long counselling journey in order to explore where these urges had originated from and what alternatives she could find in order to deal with the depths of despair and anger she felt.*

A suicidal client will invoke many feelings in the counsellor, such as extreme concern, tension, sadness, despair, fear and anger.

Even if a contract has been made between client and counsellor to the effect that the client will not harm himself or others until the next meeting (not the date of the next appointment, just in case of unavoidable cancellation, but the actual meeting of client and counsellor), there may be a tremendous sense of tension that some counsellors would not wish to undergo. Some counsellors insist on a contract with the client whereby the client promises not to commit suicide at least for the duration of counselling. There are questions of resources available to the client and how far the counsellor is prepared to go in terms of being a resource. For instance, can you offer more than a weekly session? Are you willing to give your telephone number to a client? There seems to be a tendency for the beginning counsellor to wish to 'be there' for the client even between sessions, and this may cause difficulties for the counsellor. Seasoned counsellors in agencies have often learned by bitter experience not to offer their home number as a resource for clients because, although the majority of clients will respect the counsellor's need for privacy in her own home, there are those clients who see their need as being overwhelmingly important to the extent of continuously phoning the counsellor, or even turning up at their home, until the poor counsellor feels invaded. If you are seeing clients in your own home, you might contemplate the wisdom of investing in a separate phone with an answerphone for business purposes. There is, then, the need to negotiate what is acceptable. If you are offering to be a resource it is perhaps kinder to decide beforehand when you are available to be contacted and how to be firm if the client says, 'But what happens if I want to kill myself at 4 a.m.?' It might be more useful to recommend other resources for the client, such as the Samaritans.

Although some clients will be manipulative in their use of the threat of suicide there is always the worry that one will actually kill himself. Counsellors exposed to this ordeal have described the anguished feeling of defeat and of being deskilled to the extent of seriously considering whether or not to continue being a counsellor. There is the thought of, 'Did I say or do anything to precipitate this?' or, 'Could I have done more?' and, 'Perhaps someone else would have handled it differently.' One psychologist distanced herself by saying that if the client was determined to kill himself then no-one could have stopped him. There is no doubt that a counsellor faced with this difficulty will need much support from her supervisor and colleagues.

It may be that you feel that suicidal clients represent an area in which you do not wish to work, and this decision often is taken after working with such clients. Sometimes it may help to examine your own feelings about suicide and the reasons why someone would possibly want to kill himself. Have you ever felt so full of despair that there seemed to be no other way out than killing yourself? And what helped you? One client told me that when he planned his suicide attempt he felt very calm and that it was the right decision – the only decision that could be made, because he saw no alternative. Another client found the thought of suicide comforting because it seemed that if things got too bad there was always a way out and this enabled her to carry on. Another powerful feeling can be that of anger, and the person is thinking 'I'll show them. I'll kill myself and then they will see how I've suffered and that they should have helped me.' There can also be a confusion of feeling where the person wishes to communicate but does not have the skills to do so, and this can lead to feelings of despair and frustration and a possible suicide attempt.

There is a need to understand whether suicidal thoughts are likely to lead to an actual suicide attempt. You need to establish from the client how seriously they are contemplating suicide. Ask your client. Can he or she promise not to kill themselves before the next meeting? If the client cannot make that promise, then, preferably with the client's permission, the doctor or psychiatrist should be informed and arrangements made for emergency admission to hospital.

Key practice points

1 Many clients may have suicidal thoughts but only need to talk about them.
2 Explore clients' resources in terms of available family or friends.
3 Determine the suicidal risk by asking the client if he has specific plans to kill himself.
4 It is exceedingly useful to have the name and phone number of the client's doctor or psychiatrist.

Aggressive clients
It is helpful to ascertain if the client has always been an aggressive person or if something significant has suddenly happened. The

client may recall a trigger incident, or the aggression may be a result of a stress build-up. Sometimes the client reports a childhood where aggression and violence were the norm. Occasionally, the client can identify an accident to the head which may indicate some brain damage which needs to be investigated. There is a need to determine risk to others.

> ***Example*** *A male client who went to see a counsellor showed both suicidal and extreme aggressive tendencies. He told of a horrific childhood where he was regularly beaten up by his father while his mother stood helplessly watching. He ran away at the age of fourteen and lived in an abandoned car. He was now married but the birth of a son had triggered off his own violent feelings, and he was being aggressive and threatening towards his wife. He was afraid that he might be aggressive towards his son as well, and in order to stop this he was contemplating suicide. The counsellor saw him three times in that first week, and he was able to explore his angry feelings towards his parents. His homicidal and suicidal impulses gradually faded until he felt more in control.*

In this instance the client was able to express his aggressive feelings verbally and did not need to be referred to a psychiatrist. Many aggressive thoughts can be contained within the counselling setting if we as counsellors have examined our own thoughts, feelings and concerns about this area. The client who is showing aggression may actually be feeling terrified of his or her own violent feelings. If we have examined our own aggressive and violent feelings and are not afraid of them, we can offer a secure safe place for the client to explore his or her own feelings. However, some clients will need the extra help of medication either from their doctor or from a psychiatrist, and some clients may need to be admitted to a psychiatric unit. Some practitioners may be afraid that the aggressive client may react badly to the suggestion of referral, so that is one very good reason why it is wise not to be alone in a building with a client. Some community mental health teams may offer specific groups in order to deal with anger and aggression. For some clients where the aggression is not at a violent level, assertiveness training may be of help.

> **Key practice question**
>
> Can the client learn to deal with his aggression by verbalizing his problems and using anger management, or is there a need for medication?

Psychotic problems

In your first interview with a new client you may notice possible indications of a mental illness which may need the intervention of a psychiatrist. The client may experience hallucinations, or delusions, show thought disorders such as thought blocking where there is an abrupt interruption of thoughts and which may indicate schizophrenia, there may be abnormal fluctuations of mood indicating manic-depressive disorder, or bizarre behaviours. A common indication of severe mental problems is when there is no coherent structure in the client's thoughts and the counsellor is left feeling bewildered. A client may not be aware that there is a difficulty and you may have to contact the client's doctor, preferably with the client's permission. Although there are some counsellors who specialize in working with people undergoing a psychotic episode (often because these counsellors have some psychiatric nursing background), serious mental disorders need to be assessed by a psychiatrist because sometimes psychotropic drugs or temporary hospitalization are indicated.

> ***Example*** *A counsellor saw a client who spent one and a half hours alternately crying and in deep distress and then talking in disjointed sentences about all of her life, but her thoughts were jumping so much that it was impossible to track her. The counsellor felt helpless. She also felt compassion and sensed that it was important to stay with this client and trust that she would find her own way. At the end of the session the client brightened up noticeably, gave the counsellor a wonderful smile and said, 'I feel so much better. I'm glad I saw an expert. I don't think I need to come again!' The counsellor later found out that she was under a psychiatrist and had been regularly in and out of psychiatric units.*

In this example, the counsellor quickly became aware that the client had thought disorder problems and needed to see a psychiatrist. The referral notes had not indicated any psychiatric input, and it was only when the counsellor reported back to the GP that it was revealed that this client regularly saw a psychiatrist. This referral was not appropriate for counselling although the client appeared to benefit from the one session.

Milder versions of thought disorder and personality disorders may respond to supportive counselling. Any change usually takes place over a long period of time, and there is often found to be a history of early deprivation or prolonged abuse in the client's childhood. Sometimes the client just needs to learn ways of coping with her problems and responds well to assertiveness training and general stress management. Obsessive and compulsive behaviours often respond well to cognitive and behavioural techniques in which many clinical psychologists specialize.

For further information on psychiatric issues for counsellors see Daines et al. (1997).

Key practice point

Suggest psychiatric assessment if the client is not responsive to counselling because of severe thought disorder or mood swings, hallucinations or delusions, or bizarre behaviour.

Referral for medical assessment

If you are working in a GP surgery you will have the advantage of knowing that the client has presumably been comprehensively screened for physical problems. In any other setting it is important to consider any physical conditions that might be causing or exacerbating symptoms. If you have any suspicions of possible medical problems, it is helpful to suggest that the client has a physical check-up.

In deciding whether or not the client's symptoms are predominantly psychological or medical, or a combination of both, it is useful to find out from the client when and under what circumstances the symptoms started. For example, it is well established that symptoms of tiredness, lack of concentration and subsequent depression can arise from such illnesses as glandular fever and post-viral fatigue syndrome, or myalgic encephalomyelitis (ME). There may still be a reluctance among some doctors to diagnose the latter illness, and while there is no instant cure for this debilitating problem, it is always better to know what is wrong than to be told that there is no physical problem and that it is all in one's mind. This in itself may cause frustration and depression. Of course it can be interesting to find out if there are any psychological antecedents, as in one client I saw who had been diagnosed with ME and could not continue with his high-powered job. It turned out that he had hated his job and dearly wanted to be more creative but had decided that he had to continue for financial reasons. Now he was forced to stop working and reassess his life.

Another client whom I referred back to her doctor had in fact been referred to me originally by him. However, I felt very strongly that her symptoms of tiredness, feeling cold, lack of concentration, and weight gain were not emotional but the results of a thyroid condition. (I confess that I had just read up on thyroid problems and so knew what to ask.) I did not receive a thank-you letter or acknowledgement from that particular doctor.

One of the advantages of using a formal assessment procedure such as Lazarus's Multimodal Life History Questionnaire (Lazarus, 1989: 227) is that some medical problems may come to light. The last section of the form investigates the client's health, use of drugs and environmental influences. Some drugs may affect clients, for instance Prozac given for depression may cause insomnia in some clients, so as well as ascertaining if the client is on any drugs, it is useful to have a reference book on side-effects of drugs. (*MIMS* (*Monthly Index of Medical Specialities*, published monthly by Merck Sharp and Dome, Hertford Road, Hoddesdon, Hertfordshire EN11 9BU) is given free to all doctors and would be available for reference in GP surgeries.) It is useful to be aware of other well-known effects, such as that caffeine in coffee and tea can produce anxiety symptoms.

We need to be aware of the tendency of some general practitioners to assume that a condition is psychological if no physical cause can readily be found. When I was practising as an osteopath I would have many patients saying that they must be crazy because they felt such pain and the doctor had said that there was nothing wrong. Osteopaths learn to diagnose structural anomalies that cannot be seen on X-ray, as well as medical conditions, and so are in a unique position to be able to treat neck and back problems and also many other somatic disorders. I have on occasion successfully referred a client to an osteopath when the symptoms were primarily pain or discomfort, often resulting from a car crash or accident.

In a similar way a client can misinterpret the doctor's use of the term 'psychosomatic'. A common lay interpretation is 'all in the mind', which is not helpful to the sufferer who is experiencing physical pain and discomfort. The understanding of the psychological antecedents of an illness may result in an increased ability to cope with the physical problem and a possible decrease in symptoms. If the client has primarily physical symptoms, it is always worthwhile considering stress management, which could include a recommendation to a complementary therapist such as a healer, acupuncturist, reflexologist or aromatherapist, or to yoga, tai chi or meditation classes (see Box 3.1). It is well established that an overload of stress in a person's life can result in decreased efficiency of the immune system, which can result in many different kinds of illnesses (Fontana, 1989).

For further information on medical issues for counsellors see Daines et al. (1997).

Key practice points

1   It is worth referring the client to his doctor if there are indications of a physical reason for, for instance, tiredness or various bodily pains.
2   A complementary therapist may be able to provide relief to the client's physical body while counselling tends to the client's mental and emotional well-being.

Referral to a community mental health team

The community mental health teams (CMHTs) usually consist of a variety of mental health workers and often include clinical psychologists, counselling psychologists, counsellors, psychotherapists, community psychiatric nurses and specialist nurse practitioners. There would be strong links with the psychiatric services and the social services. Your client would need to see his general practitioner in order to be referred to a community mental health team. Your client may ask you to send a letter to his doctor in order to strengthen his request (see Appendix 2). This is an excellent

---

Box 3.1   Complementary therapies

- *Acupuncture* – uses needles in the skin at specific points in order to regulate the energy flow in the body.
- *Alexander Technique* – becoming aware of, and adjusting habitual patterns of posture and movement which can cause tension both physically and mentally.
- *Aromatherapy* – massage using essential oils extracted from plants.
- *Bach flower remedies* – used to balance emotional states and promote well-being; 'rescue remedy' for panic states.
- *Chiropractic* – manipulation, especially of the spine, in order to restore pain-free function and movement.
- *Spiritual healing* – laying-on of hands, either touching the body or working on the aura around the body, to help physical, mental, emotional and spiritual difficulties.
- *Herbalism* – herbal medicines used to treat most illnesses of body and mind.
- *Homeopathy* – minute doses of substances that can stimulate the individual's own healing mechanism.
- *Naturopathy* – looking at all aspects of a person's life, physical, mental, emotional and spiritual, and restoring balance using diet, exercise, relaxation and gentle manipulation.
- *Osteopathy* – rhythmic stretching, articulation and manipulation of the spine and other parts of the body in order to restore pain-free function and movement.
- *Reflexology* – massage of reflex points of the feet in order to release tensions and imbalances in other parts of the body.

---

opportunity to make yourself known to the general practitioner. The CMHT may offer a variety of groups including assertiveness, anger management, anxiety management, and treatment for eating disorders. There will also be a variety of specialist services which may include family therapy, couple counselling and child psychotherapy. Sometimes members of the team may offer counselling within local surgeries.

Key practice point

The community mental health teams can be accessed through the GP and may be able to provide counselling and specialist treatments from various practitioners, and may run groups dealing with specific areas of difficulty.

Box 3.2   Definitions of mental health professionals

- *Psychiatrist*   A psychiatrist is a medically qualified practitioner who specializes in the diagnosis and treatment of people who are mentally ill. Psychiatrists are expert in the use of drug treatments. Some psychiatrists may also practise psychotherapy. The GP can refer people to a psychiatrist.

- *Clinical psychologist*   A clinical psychologist is someone who has a psychology degree and has then undertaken a postgraduate qualification in clinical psychology. A clinical psychologist may use psychological tests for assessment purposes. They are specialists in psychological therapies such as cognitive and behavioural and other psychotherapies. They may be able to offer specific treatments such as eye movement desensitization therapy for post-traumatic disorder. Clinical psychologists are based in hospitals, mental health centres, or may see people privately.

- *Counselling psychologist*   A counselling psychologist is someone who has a psychology degree and has then undertaken a postgraduate qualification in counselling. They are general counsellors with a psychological background who may be able to offer various specialities such as stress management. They often work within the community mental health teams or privately.

- *Community psychiatric nurses (CPNS)*   CPNs are experienced psychiatric nurses who work with people in the community and are often part of a community mental health team. A CPN can visit people in their own homes and provide support and advice on various aspects of mental health. They may or may not have training in psychotherapy or counselling. Sometimes they have particular training in specialist areas such as eating disorders or agoraphobia.

- *Psychotherapist*   Psychotherapists have varying levels of training. There is now the United Kingdom Council for Psychotherapy (UKCP) which is a register for psychotherapists who have reached the required standard. Many psychotherapists work from a psychodynamic perspective, but there are other orientations as well, such as cognitive-behavioural and transactional analysis. Psychotherapists may work in various settings including community mental health teams or work privately.

- *Psychoanalyst*   Psychoanalysts undergo many years of training involving extensive psychoanalysis for the trainee. Normally, they do private work because of the extensive and expensive therapy offered.

- *Counsellor*   Counsellors have varying levels of training. There is now BAC Accreditation status with the British Association for Counselling and the United Kindom Register of Counsellors which indicates a high standard of training and experience. Counsellors may work from a psychodynamic, humanistic, cognitive-behavioural or transpersonal perspective. Counsellors may work in various settings including community mental health teams, agencies, educational settings, work settings, or may practise privately.

Summary

1 Clients presenting with psychosis, suicidal or aggressive impulses may need psychiatric evaluation. Some clients may benefit from psychotropic medication.
2 The client's symptoms may be due to a physical problem. Also be aware of the side-effects of prescribed drugs.
3 It is important to be broadly aware of different therapeutic professionals and their areas of expertise.

4

Alternative Counselling Referrals

There are various forms of counselling that may be suitable for a particular client and that we need to have details about. The client may benefit more from group, family or couple counselling, or a different counselling orientation, or may wish to see a counsellor of particular gender, race, religion or sexual orientation. The client may need either time-limited counselling or long-term counselling or may need guidance finding free counselling.

Referrals for group, family or couple counselling

At the beginning of counselling or after some individual counselling, it may become evident that the client needs more than can be offered in individual counselling. Some clients would never wish to enter a group situation while others find immense benefit from group counselling. Some clients need to have the whole family involved and some need to have counselling with their partner.

Group counselling

Individual therapists, groups of therapists, or the community mental health team in your area may offer various counselling groups. Groups start up at varying times and so a constant up-date is needed to keep track. Groups may run from GP surgeries or hospitals or health centres. Groups may be for general counselling, or more specific areas such as stress management, anxiety, assertiveness, anger, sexual abuse, eating disorders or addictions. Clients may feel anxiety initially at the idea of a group, but usually the relief that they are not alone with their problem easily outweighs that first apprehension. They often find that in a group environment with shared experiences they can more easily form relationships. The client may or may not wish to have individual counselling at the same time as attending the group.

There are specific advantages of group therapy that you may wish to consider when possibly recommending this form of counselling to your clients. Apart from the powerful realization that they are not alone with their particular problem, the therapy group may offer acceptance and belonging, insight from interpersonal exploration and observation, hope and problem-solving, helping others, and catharsis (Dryden and Feltham, 1994). Some clients may wish to take advantage of the possibilities of personal growth and development that can take place within particular groups such as encounter groups, psychodrama, or gestalt or transactional analysis groups.

Group work is not beneficial for those clients who are too apprehensive to respond to group pressures. Such clients would either hide themselves within the group or would be too anxious to attend. However, what seems an impossible idea to a client at the beginning of individual counselling may be more appealing towards the end of counselling when he or she is more confident.

Groups are often self-referring, like Alcoholics Anonymous, in which case the client can approach the group directly. If the groups are run within the health service, the client would need to approach their general practitioner in order to be referred to a particular group.

Family counselling

Occasionally there are clients whose problems appear to be interwoven with the family situation and the whole family needs to be seen. This is often the case when a child or young teenager presents with behavioural problems or eating disorders. It has been found that the client with the presenting problem is often not the sickest member of the family 'but is protecting more vulnerable members, or the stability of the marriage, by "volunteering" to be the symptom carrier, scapegoat, or rescuer'

(Skynner and Brown, 1981). You as counsellor need to recognize that your client's problems are being maintained by the family and that your client will frequently talk about his or her involvement with family members. A possible difficulty with individual counselling could be that the negative influences of the family undo any advances made by the client. Another possible arena for family therapy is that of complicated bereavement (Worden, 1991).

Often the whole family is seen by two or more therapists and the sessions may be recorded so that the complex patterns of the family members can be seen and analysed. Sometimes change can occur within one session, and usually within six sessions. Family therapists have found that spacing sessions a month apart can increase the rate of change (Skynner, 1969). A referral needs to be made to the nearest family therapy centre, and this may be either self-referral or through the general practitioner. There are often waiting lists for this form of therapy. In London the Institute of Family Therapy (see Chapter 9 for more details) offers family therapy, and self-referral is possible.

Couple counselling

A client may present with relationship problems, and it can sometimes be quickly established that both partners need to be seen together. Some counsellors have gained the appropriate training to counsel couples, but it can be difficult if you have seen one partner for some time, as the other partner may be apprehensive, jealous or resentful of the relationship already established. Some counsellors may offer to see the client and his or her partner for one session in order to assess the situation, but it is usually easier to refer to a colleague or to Relate for couple counselling. It is possible for clients to contact Relate directly (see Chapter 9 for more details). The waiting list varies from region to region, and a donation fee is often expected. In London the Institute of Family Therapy also offers couple therapy and is self-referring.

Sometimes one partner does not wish to partake of couple therapy, as the following vignette exemplifies.

Example   *A counsellor was involved in an interesting situation when she saw a man for individual counselling* *and a colleague saw the wife. Both the colleague and his client wanted a 'foursome' so that the relationship could be explored. The problem was that the husband did not want this arrangement, because in individual counselling he had explored various issues that he wished to keep secret from his wife. The counsellor of the husband also did not want a foursome arrangement, because she knew that her client did not wish to be totally honest and open. The husband eventually side-stepped the issue by initiating a temporary separation. Both husband and wife continued with individual counselling and eventually went back together. In this instance one of the partners was worried that some confidential secrets might inadvertently be talked about.*

Sometimes useful work can be done if the partner of your client wishes to join in the occasional session in order to help the client. Several times I have found that the interaction between the client and their partner has illuminated a particular difficulty that the client has. For example, one client was experiencing severe depressions, and it was only after her partner had agreed to attend a session that it was revealed that he was always particularly caring at these times and, the more vulnerable the client was, the more loving he became. It was helpful for my client to explore other ways of asking for and receiving this loving attention.

Key practice points

1 Group therapy could be indicated for a client who would benefit from the sharing, understanding and support that a group can supply.
2 Family therapy can be useful if the client's problems are being maintained by the family.
3 Couple therapy is indicated if the client's problems are focused on his or her relationship with his or her partner.

Referral to a different counselling orientation

It may be helpful to summarize very briefly some of the main counselling orientations. In general the research into the effectiveness of therapy has shown a general equivalence of outcome

(Smith et al., 1980), with the therapist's characteristics of empathy and commitment being shown to indicate the most favourable outcome (Orlinsky and Howard, 1986). However, you may feel that your client needs a different or more specialized approach for a particular difficulty. For further information on the main therapies refer to Dryden (1996), and for the innovative therapies see Rowan and Dryden (1988).

Person-centred approach

The person-centred counsellor uses the approach originally advocated by Carl Rogers. The counsellor believes that every person has the resources within himself to deal with his own problems and development and that access to these resources can be facilitated by certain conditions. If the counsellor can show the client unconditional positive regard, hopefully he will feel safe enough to explore all parts of himself without the fear of judgement. If accurate empathy is shown by the counsellor, the client feels understood. The third condition is that of the genuineness of the counsellor, who presents herself as an equal rather than hiding behind the mask of 'the expert'. Within the safety and acceptance of this counselling relationship the client can explore his true feelings and get in touch with his inner self. A person-centred counsellor would probably see the limitations of this approach only in terms of the limitations of particular counsellors. To be a person-centred counsellor means that the counsellor ideally needs to know all aspects of herself, on all levels, her physical, mental, emotional and spiritual components. The person-centred counsellor needs to be open and flexible, willing to learn and grow. It can be a tough discipline but immensely rewarding.

Person-centred counsellors do not diagnose and would probably take on most people for counselling, believing in the healing potential of the counselling relationship. This approach is thought to be particularly good for any client who does not wish to be directed and guided by the counsellor, and for those clients who are especially vulnerable because of bereavement or childhood deprivation.

Cognitive-behavioural approach

The cognitive-behavioural approach is one of exploring how the client's counterproductive ways of thinking and behaving have contributed to his problems and looking at ways of changing these. The cognitive counsellor will examine the client's typical and unhelpful ways of thinking about events and will help the client to challenge irrational ways of thinking. Some of these patterns of thinking may come from childhood and so need constant challenging until the client can think differently about certain situations and behave accordingly.

The behavioural approach is one of utilizing many methods, including relaxation, desensitization and so on, in order to cope with stressful situations, phobias and compulsions affecting the client's life. Other behavioural methods might include assertiveness training, social skills training, and the use of rewards for desirable behaviour. Clinical psychologists, and specialist nurse practitioners, as well as some counsellors, may be skilled in behavioural therapy.

The emphasis in the cognitive-behavioural approach is one of helping the client to develop life-skills in order to cope better in his life situation. It could be particularly suitable for depression, anxiety, phobias and obsessive-compulsive disorder, but probably not for personal growth.

Psychodynamic approach

The psychodynamic approach is one of exploration of childhood events or chronic intrapsychic patterns and their harmful repetition in daily life, in order to discover why particular problems have arisen. Psychological illness is seen as an inability to manage inner states of conflict. The counsellor has been trained to be aware of defences that came into being in order to suppress unacceptable ideas and feelings and to be able to interpret and work through these, following the theories laid down originally by Freud and adapted and developed by other psychoanalytic practitioners and theorists. Techniques may include encouragement of free association, the interpretation of dreams and the analysis of transference in order for the unconscious material to be made conscious. The theories of Freud, Klein and Jung are examined succinctly under 'psychodynamic therapy' in Dryden (1996).

This approach may be especially suitable for those clients who wish to explore their childhood experiences in depth in order to understand their possibly complex problems. It is normally seen as a long-term therapy, and the client may be seen several times a week for months or years. It is not suitable for clients who wish to get rid of their symptoms quickly without necessarily understanding the causes.

Transactional analysis

Transactional analysis was developed by Eric Berne and is regarded by some as a cognitive approach in that it analyses the way clients interpret the world, although because Berne believed that everyone has an inner drive for health, this would indicate a humanistic position. Berne's belief in the fundamental worth of the human being is shown by the concept of 'OK-ness', particularly the 'I'm OK – You're OK' position. Transactional analysis uses the idea of 'parent, adult and child' ego states. The client may not be aware of the 'messages' from authority figures that have pervaded his childhood and that have not only formed the way he sees himself and his situation but may be disturbing his adult functioning. Through the awareness of his typical patterns of interactions with other people, the client can beneficially change the way he reacts to people and situations. This approach is particularly good for clients who enjoy analysing their thoughts and patterns of behaviour.

Gestalt approaches

Gestalt therapy is associated with Fritz Perls, who believed that every individual strives for self-actualization. Perls was interested in disturbances of clients' interactions with their environment that prevented a full awareness and enjoyment of life. Gestalt counselling is often concerned with the 'here and now' interaction between counsellor and client in order to heighten the client's awareness. The approach can be a hard-hitting one which is often used with clients who have already undergone some kind of counselling and are interested in exploring their feelings and personal interactions in greater depth. Some of the Gestalt techniques, such as the 'two-chair' or empty chair technique, are used eclectically within other orientations. The Gestalt therapist tends to be somewhat directive but not interpretative and encourages the client to take responsibility for himself.

Body–work approaches

There are some counsellors who specialize in body work with their clients, and this may be especially useful for those clients who find it difficult to verbally express feelings and may experience physical discomfort and pain. When the body tensions are released, the client may then become aware of forgotten experiences and the feelings involved. There is biodynamic therapy according to which mind, body and spirit are totally interfused and tension locked in the body will prevent a full expression of well-being, and therapists combine psychotherapy and massage. Some counsellors incorporate massage, aromatherapy or healing in their repertoire. Sometimes it is helpful for the client to be referred to a counsellor who works on a more physical level to enable deep tensions to be released. It is possible that feelings and memories can 'flood' out and threaten to overwhelm the client, and so extra therapeutic time should be made available to deal with this situation if it arises. And of course some clients have problems with touch and so a body–work approach would not be suitable at the beginning of their therapeutic journey, although later on it could be helpful for a client to receive non-threatening touch.

Spiritual approaches
Pyschosynthesis was founded by Roberto Assagioli (Assagioli, 1965), who was concerned not only with the solution of everyday personal problems, but also with human potential. Psychosynthesis uses the idea of centring in order to contact the higher self, or superconscious, which is a source of wisdom and harmony. Some of the techniques that may be used by a counsellor include subpersonality recognition, understanding the transference, imagery work and visualization, in order for the client to understand the part of himself that is trying to emerge from the difficulty he is experiencing.

Transpersonal counselling is an umbrella term that includes work by Jung, Assagioli, Frankl, Maslow, Grof, Wilbur and Fadiman and looks at the more spiritual approaches to problems and dissatisfaction with life (Rowan, 1993). The transpersonal counsellor may use a variety of methods, including relaxation, meditation, visualization, symbolic languages, dreamwork, imaging or healing. A problem in life is seen as an opportunity to learn and grow.

The spiritual approaches are particularly indicated for those clients who are searching for a meaning for their lives, who wish to release their creative energies and take charge of their lives.

Those clients who have more concrete problems, such as particular decisions to make, and who are not familiar with visualization or creative work might find the approach bewildering.

Eclectic and integrative counselling
Eclectic counsellors draw on several different orientations in order to be able to offer different, tailored approaches to individual clients. Many eclectic counsellors will use a base model like Egan's three-stage approach which uses exploration followed by problem-solving (Egan, 1994) or Lazarus's Multimodal Model which systematically explores the client's behaviour, affect, sensation, imagery, cognition, interpersonal relationships, health and lifestyle factors (Lazarus, 1989). The eclectic counsellor will explore other models and orientations in order to expand her expertise and be able to draw on more techniques to use with particular clients. If an eclectic counsellor does not have a base model or an understanding of the importance of the therapeutic alliance and common therapeutic variables then there could be a danger of a haphazard approach with no solid foundation (Dryden, 1989).

Integrative counsellors often use a counselling approach which brings together the therapeutic factors which are common to most counselling orientations. These include: the therapist–client relationship; interpretation, insight and understanding; catharsis, emotional expression and release; relaxation; information; reassurance and support; modelling; confronting one's problems; clarifying and modifying client expectancies and providing both a credible therapeutic framework for the client's problems and a credible rationale for treatment (Garfield, 1982). This unification of common factors means that integrationism rests on a sound empirical base and gives a framework that can embrace other developments in counselling approaches (Culley, 1991).

Another view of integrative counselling is where a practitioner studies two or more orientations in depth and integrates these together. For instance, there is cognitive-analytic therapy (CAT) which was created by Anthony Ryle (1991) from elements of personal construct theory and object relations theory. CAT is an integrative model of therapy which combines understanding thought patterns and behaviour with the insight of psychodynamic explanations. It is used as a time-limited model.

> **Key practice point**
>
> Whether we have been trained in one kind of counselling theory or whether we are eclectic counsellors, there are occasions when a client would benefit from referral to a counsellor specializing in a particular counselling orientation, because of the particular nature of the client's problems or needs.

Referral to a counsellor of particular gender, race, religion or sexual orientation

The client may prefer a counsellor of a particular gender, race, religion or sexual orientation. Community Mental Health Teams and other organizations usually try to employ both male and female practitioners and, if at all possible, practitioners of different races. In some areas of the country there are voluntary counselling centres that provide for ethnic minorities with counsellors who are fluent in different languages. If the client specifically wishes to see a counsellor from a particular religious background, it may be necessary for a client to seek advice from their own religious organization. Likewise if the client specifically wishes to see someone of their own sexual orientation, there may be a suitable local counselling organization or it may be possible to gain some information from the national organizations concerned with sexuality issues.

There are many female clients who prefer to see a female counsellor. Often this is because the problem is specifically to do with being a woman and some clients may not feel that a man could understand their problems. Many clients say, 'I know you understand because you are a woman.' Also if a woman has been sexually attacked by a man, it may feel impossible to talk about this to a man, especially alone in a room with one. Sometimes it could be beneficial for a woman to have a safe nurturing experience with a male counsellor if this can be arranged after the raw material has been worked through. Some male counsellors have specialized in counselling in sensitive areas such as rape or childhood sexual abuse but they are also aware of the importance to the woman of having a choice of male or female counsellor. As with male nurses and midwives, what is ultimately important is the person and his abilities rather than his gender, but for a woman who feels threatened by a male presence the gender is of utmost importance even if they have to be on a waiting list for a long time.

Similarly, there are some male clients who prefer to see a male counsellor. A male colleague of mine sometimes hears 'I know you understand because you are a man' from his male clients. It seems that the shared experience of maleness or femaleness can be of fundamental importance to a client.

Apart from the obvious advantage of communicating in the same language, there are cultural differences amongst different races. Body language and emotional expression may be different in different cultures. For instance, in some cultures it may not be polite to maintain eye contact, especially between opposite sexes, and this could cause misunderstandings. In some cultures there is intense loyalty to the family and family vaues and seeking counselling could be construed as betrayal. The client may prefer to work with a counsellor of the same race because of their common background and understanding, for instance if there is an expectation of arranged marriages. If it is not possible to refer the client, or the client is happy to work with you, it is usually best to confess one's lack of familiarity with their culture if this is the case (Dryden and Feltham, 1994). It is essential for counsellors to fully explore their own prejudices as regards racism, since unconscious perceptions will influence the counsellor's behaviour and responses (Lago and Thompson, 1989).

Sometimes when working with a client it becomes evident that some of their difficulties may arise from their religious upbringing. Occasionally, it may be more sensitive to the client's needs if a referral is made to a counsellor who has specialized in religious issues. This may be a Christian counsellor if the client is having difficulties dealing with conflicts that arise from their Christian beliefs, or similarly for other religions. Sometimes if the client has had difficulties with a fundamentalist background he might need a counsellor who is not overtly religious. If a client has exited from a cult he may benefit from seeing someone who has the relevant knowledge.

Sexual orientation may be a problem for a client, especially if he or she is experiencing problems with social acceptance of homosexuality. A client may find that he or she feels more at ease with a counsellor who also has gone through a similar experience with friends and family, and so a referral to a Gay and Lesbian Counselling Service might be beneficial. Some counsellors may feel that they cannot congruently counsel practising homosexuals, because of conflicting religious beliefs. Obviously, as counsellors, we need to be fully aware of any prejudices that we might hold, in order that we do not damage our clients. We need to be aware of our limitations and 'any reasons at all why you may feel that your value systems or beliefs might make it difficult for you to offer an open and respectful relationship to your client, which is affirming of their lifestyle choices' (Davies and Neal, 1996: 195). If we know that we cannot work with someone because of conflicting beliefs, then it is ethical to refer to another counsellor.

> ***Example***   *A gay man sought counselling from an organization that offered counselling for gay men and lesbians who were experiencing difficulties. He explained to this new counsellor that he had seen someone before who stated that his wish to express his homosexuality was a moral problem. He did not return to this particular counsellor but was left not only with his original problems but also now feeling even more unacceptable. His new counsellor was able not only to accept him as a person but also to fully accept his homosexuality. This helped the client to let go of the shame that he had been holding and reaffirm his belief in himself.*

Leitman (1995) argues the need for gay-affirmative therapy. He believes that some counsellors pathologize homosexuality or believe that it signifies an emotional developmental problem. If a heterosexual counsellor believes that homosexuality is as valid as heterosexuality then, Leitman states, such a person could offer gay-affirmative therapy. Even homosexual counsellors could have problems if they have not worked through their own 'internalised homophobia' (Leitman, 1995).

Key practice point

A client may prefer to choose a male or female counsellor, a counsellor of the same race, the same religion or the same sexuality because of the immediate empathy that can often be present when two people have similar experiences.

Referral for free counselling

If you are working privately as a counsellor, it may happen that you may sometimes see a client who does not realize the financial commitment of counselling. It may be that the client assumed that he would only need a few sessions, when it is probable that he needs a lot longer. Some counsellors have a sliding scale for clients, and others may accept services in exchange for counselling, but it is unusual to provide free counselling if that is your main source of income. It might be that you need to direct the client towards free or low-cost counselling services.

Free counselling may be available in some doctors' surgeries, from mental health teams, social services, student counselling services, Employee Assistance Programmes (EAPs), religious organizations or from voluntary agencies. Sometimes the waiting lists are long, and people may have to wait many weeks or even months. This is especially so for evening or weekend appointments. Some surgeries or agencies may provide a certain number of sessions free and then expect some payment from the clients. Some EAPs will provide limited but prompt counselling for employees and often for family members as well. When you are doing your research for facilities to recommend to clients it is useful to discover the qualifications of the counsellors because, although most organizations offering counselling are looking for counsellors who are accredited with BAC, the demand is such that the counsellor sometimes may not in fact have many qualifications or much experience. It may be that the counsellor in the doctor's surgery or agency is a counsellor-in-training, which should be made clear to the client and is often acceptable because of the close supervision that is given to the trainee. During the years I have been training counsellors I have not been aware of any client who has shunned a counsellor because she has been in training.

Key practice point

It is a good idea to explore the forms of free or low-cost counselling that exist in your area for clients who cannot afford private counselling.

Self-help and mutual-aid groups

Sometimes the client presents with a problem and you have the information on a local self-help group that deals with this problem. Many groups tend to wax and wane, appear and disappear, depending on the needs of the local people and on funding, but are often advertised in health centres or libraries. There may be groups dealing with bereavement, cancer and other severe health problems, carers, victims of crime, substance abuse, sexual abuse, depression, post-natal depression and eating problems. Some of these groups are extremely helpful, supportive and informative while others may become unhelpful for some clients because, as one client stated, 'They all sat around and moaned.' Some people are helped just by knowing that there are others with similar problems. Some clients find that they feel better because they can help other people by sharing experiences. Some 'mutual-aid' groups, such as Alcoholics Anonymous, are well established throughout the country and offer understanding from other recovering alcoholics and a support system for the sufferer and their family. Some clients would choose to attend a self-help group at the same time as receiving counselling.

Key practice point

Self-help groups can be supportive for a client and/or a client's family, and it is worth advising clients about them when appropriate.

Long-term counselling

Entrenched psychological problems that originate from childhood experiences may need long-term work. The clients who will benefit from long-term counselling are those who are motivated to explore their emotional selves in depth, have a degree of insight, and wish to understand the causes of their problems. Clients who present with many difficulties that have no clear focus and which may have their origins in childhood experiences, will need time to explore their past and how their thoughts, emotions and behaviour have been shaped, and recurring distressful patterns formed. Clients presenting with certain problems such as addictions, childhood sexual abuse, severe depression, chronic obsessional symptoms, eating disorders, suicide attempts or borderline personality disorder will often need long-term counselling. Also people who wish to explore their past in depth for personal growth and understanding will need counselling over a long period of time. For more detailed information see *Long-Term Counselling* by Shipton and Smith (1998).

Bloch (1979), in his paper on assessment of patients for long-term psychotherapy (or counselling), concluded that the following factors were indicative of a favourable outcome:

1 a reasonable level of personality integration and general functioning
2 motivation for change
3 realistic expectations of the therapeutic process
4 at least average intelligence
5 non-psychotic conditions
6 the presence of strong affect like anxiety and depression at the time of assessment
7 life circumstances free of any unresolvable crises.

Key practice point

There will always be some clients who need a long-term relationship with a counsellor in order to build the security and trust needed to explore their difficulties and enhance the quality of their lives.

Time-limited counselling

Time-limited counselling may consist of a planned single session (Talmon, 1990) or up to thirty sessions (Malan, 1979). Most time-limited work, particularly for Employee Assistance Programmes (EAPs) and the National Health Service, seems to be around five to ten sessions. The sort of clients who would benefit from time-limited counselling are those who are motivated and whose problem is clearly identifiable, not severe or chronic, and allows for therapeutic focusing. The sort of problems that may respond to short-term intervention include anxiety and stress management, mild depression, bereavement, simple phobias, assertiveness, career decisions, and some relationship difficulties. However, time-limited therapy has also been used for personality disorders in cognitive-analytic therapy which offers sixteen sessions (Ryle, 1991), and brief therapy has been successfully used for addictions (Van Bilsen, 1996). Most counsellors would agree that it is not so much the presenting problem that determines the length of counselling needed, as the motivation and determination of the client. For more detailed information on time-limited counselling see *Time-Limited Counselling* by Colin Feltham (1997).

Key practice point

Time-limited counselling is particularly useful for clients who are well motivated and whose problems can be easily identified, and where focused work can be used successfully.

Summary

1 Group, family or couple counselling may be indicated at the first assessment of the client, or later after some individual counselling.

2 Some clients may benefit from a specific approach to counselling – for instance a 'thinking' client may respond more favourably to cognitive therapy, a 'feeling' client to a humanistic approach, an 'action' client to a problem-solving approach. Also some client problems may respond to a particular counselling approach.

3 A client may prefer to see a counsellor of a particular gender, race, religion or sexuality.

4 Self-help groups may give the client extra support.

5 Long-term counselling is indicated for long-standing psychological problems which would benefit from in-depth work.

6 Time-limited counselling is particularly beneficial for focused problem-solving work by motivated clients.

5

Referral Issues in the Middle Phase

In the middle phase of counselling some problems may necessitate the referral of a client to another counsellor. Some of these problems, such as transference or counter-transference issues, may be resolved with discussion with a counselling supervisor. Other, more practical problems such as the counsellor or client moving from the area, will involve a premature termination and possible referral.

Possible problems with transference or counter-transference issues

Transference occurs when clients have strong feelings towards the counsellor which originate from the client's own unconscious conflicts. Hence these feelings and thoughts towards the counsellor can be of immense value in the unravelling of the client's problems. The task for the counsellor is firstly one of recognition that these feelings and thoughts are stronger than is warranted by the immediate situation, then to help the client understand and work through them. If the counsellor fails to recognize that transference is taking place, then the counselling may become stuck with either strong positive feelings from the client, such as love, or strong negative feelings such as anger, hate or fear. The counsellor will usually realize what is happening for the client, and progress is made, but occasionally a referral to another practitioner may be advisable if the situation is seemingly unresolvable.

Example *A client was having problems recognizing and dealing with anger. She had recounted the physical abuse she had experienced from her mother and the difficulties she was having with her own daughter. There was a lot of hidden anger shown in her behaviour which included abuse of alcohol, shop-lifting offences, storming out of jobs, and involvement in abusive relationships with men. At one point in a session she suddenly eyed a heavy paperweight and said, 'I could hit you with that before anyone could stop me.' As this seemed to come completely out of the blue the counsellor felt quite bewildered and said nothing. The client then said, 'Well why aren't you scared? I landed my mother in hospital.' There was a distinct threat in her voice and stance. Fortunately the counsellor noticed a toy squeaky hammer nearby and said creatively and humorously, 'I'm not scared because I can defend myself with that hammer.' The client burst out laughing. Perhaps the moral of that story is to hide paperweights but keep toy squeaky hammers handy! (Obviously, more subtle and non-humorous responses will usually be needed.) Fortunately the outcome in this case was positive in that the client was able to talk about the anger she felt towards her mother and explore the underlying low opinion she had about herself.*

In this instance it was valuable to stay calm so that the anger situation could be defused. The anger the client displayed was not a reflection of the actual interactions between the counsellor and client, but rather a transference situation in that the client needed to express the anger she felt towards her physically abusive mother. If the counsellor can see the situation as a potential breakthrough and can avoid feeling defensive, the value for the client may be enormous. Difficulties can arise if the counsellor takes the anger or criticism personally. Sometimes the client can take something that has happened during the session and magnify it out of all proportion and this is a signal that there is an underlying issue for the client that needs to be highlighted.

A counsellor related the following experience of counter-transference that she did not recognize until the supervisor pointed out what was happening.

Example When I was training I had a client who was feeling hopeless and helpless after losing his wife, his house and his highly paid job. He could only see a blackness ahead of himself and a fast descent towards the gutter. During counselling he explored his situation and how he had allowed it to happen and he was able to grieve for his losses. At this turning point some complications arose for the counselling relationship. As this client was able to let go of the hopelessness, he revealed the power of his personality and his need to control whatever situation he found himself in. He became seductive. Fortunately, because I was in training, all the sessions were recorded, and when my supervisor heard a particular tape he said, with incredulity strong in his voice, 'You're flirting with him!' 'Oh no I'm not!' I replied heatedly. However, upon listening to the tape carefully, it became evident that, in order to assert his power my client was using his sexuality and I was unconsciously responding to it. With subsequent awareness of what was happening I was able to help this client explore how he was using his sexuality in order to be in control of women and how he might instead use his considerable charm in a more productive way for himself and his partners.

In this example the client indicated one of his problems: that of relating meaningfully to women. He apparently had no difficulties with sex itself but could not share himself emotionally. He told the counsellor later that he had had affairs with women in the health professions. It needed someone to be objective enough to help him see what he was doing and how he could change things. This client had acted out his problem, with all the attendant feelings, in the counselling situation and, once it was recognized, it was possible to use this transference in order to help the client see everything more clearly. An obvious problem that can arise for the counsellor is when the objectivity is lost and the situation is taken at face value.

A client often brings extremely strong feelings, such as anger, hate, fear, sadness and love, into the counselling sessions. Some of these feelings may be directed at the counsellor. The counsellor has the task of helping the client to sort out what is an appropriate reaction within the present relationship between counsellor and client and what may indicate a long-standing problem from the past. The client may never have learnt how to manage strong emotions because the parents may have been emotionally unavailable and/or used the child as a depository for their own anger and pain. The counsellor needs to be able to be an emotional 'container' for the client: 'by staying calm and reasonable in the presence of strong emotions, the therapist becomes a healthy model' (Delvey, 1985), and so the client realizes that these feelings can be managed.

Counter-transference manifests when the counsellor experiences strong feelings that are not justified by the counselling situation and finds herself acting out of character. Mark Aveline warns that counter-transference problems are recognized by 'intensifications or departures from the therapist's usual practice' (Aveline, 1993: 324). At the time it may be easy to justify this uncharacteristic behaviour, but upon examination the unhelpful nature of these behaviours can be seen. Counsellors need to be very aware of their normal thoughts, feelings and behaviour in situations so that any deviation can be picked up. Sometimes the counsellor may experience an uneasiness about the situation and the whole picture is not revealed until there is a chance to explore everything thoroughly in counselling supervision. The counsellor needs to become aware of her own instincts of 'something not quite right', and this 'warning bell' may take the form of a particular body tension, for instance in the back of the neck or shoulders, or a feeling of uneasiness and possibly anxiety. If the counsellor can become aware of her own warning reactions it may be possible to identify the problem immediately and act upon it.

Counter-transference indicates something about the client that can be worked upon within the counselling session, or a problem for the counsellor that needs to be worked on in counselling supervision or personal counselling, or both situations may apply. If as counsellors we find ourselves 'overreacting' with a particular client, it is most likely that the client's problem is being unconsciously re-worked in the counselling setting. If for instance we find ourselves feeling excessively protective towards a particular client, it may be that this client has a strong desire for a parent-figure, having not experienced this before, or conversely the client may have overprotective parents. Herein lies a potential danger of acting on our feelings without reflection, because the client may then be prevented from exploring his own feelings of loss regarding inadequate parenting or anger at the restrictions imposed by overprotection. If a counsellor can share her own feelings directly with the client this may enable the client to identify the problem. Sometimes it may be that the feelings we have towards the client are those that others have also, and it can be useful to share these feelings at the appropriate time. If the strong feelings we experience as counsellors do not belong to the client's situation, then we need to explore our own inner world to discover if the client has triggered anything for us.

> ***Example***   *A client presented with intense anger and hatred towards her prospective daughter-in-law. The counsellor used empathic responding in order to help the client explore the situation but knew that she needed to take this to supervision because of her own intense feelings of dislike for the client. In supervision it was realized that the counsellor was in fact reminded of her own mother-in-law who had very strong views and could be stubborn and intractable. What was fascinating about this situation was that the supervisor instantly recognized that this client reminded him of his own mother-in-law! Having identified what the counter-transference problems were for the counsellor, the coun-selling progressed to a satisfactory conclusion for the client in that she could express her feelings and explore her views in her own way.*

Occasionally, it is not possible for the counsellor to identify and work through a negative counter-transference while seeing the client, and a referral is needed in order to protect the client. The counsellor's responsibility is to recognize what is happening and take it to supervision, and the supervisor's responsibility is to assess the situation to determine whether or not a referral is necessary. Watkins (1989) identifies four counter-transference styles that may interfere with the counselling. These four styles result in overprotective behaviour, benign behaviour, rejecting behaviour or hostile behaviour. Overprotective behaviour on the part of the counsellor may infantilize the client and induce dependency. Benign counter-transference may result in a mutual sharing and friendship, with exploration of the client's concerns lacking any depth. Rejecting counter-transference may result from the counsellor's fear of demands from others, and the counsellor may act coldly and distantly and increase any client fears of abandonment by the unnecessary use of silence or sharp interventions. Hostile counter-transference behaviour by the counsellor can result from either seeing something in the client that the counsellor dislikes, or being afraid of being infected by the client's problems, and can result in abusive verbal responses or in consistently being late or missing appointments. The client may be seriously harmed by these forms of counter-transference and lose trust and feel traumatized.

Example *A client was able to describe her experiences to a counsellor only after a period of several years because her trust in counselling had almost been totally destroyed. The client presented as a timid, dependent personality with difficulty separating her own mental processes and emotions from other people's. For instance, if she went into a room full of people, apart from feeling self-conscious and thinking that everyone was looking at her, she would pick up the feelings around her and might descend into a state of depression because someone in the room was depressed. Unfortunately for this client it seemed that she was particularly susceptible to the more negative emotions. It appeared that the original counsellor had firstly been overprotective and benign in that there were lots of hugs and self-disclosure and not much counselling in any depth. Then when the client appeared to be taking on board some of the counsellor's problems the counsellor became rejecting and hostile. There was a sudden withdrawal of all physical contact, a refusal to discuss any difficulties in the relationship, angry responses and an emotional distancing. The client ended the counselling because she felt that this was not helpful to her. She was left with increased anxiety and depression which eventually drove her to find more help. The new counsellor fortunately had considerable experience, had worked with various kinds of personality disorder, and used her own indignation at the original counsellor's behaviour to help forge a strong rapport with this client in the first session, mainly by describing her own anger for the way this client had been treated. This helped establish trust because the client had felt that the first counsellor had been angry at her, and the client had never experienced the relief of anyone feeling angry for her. This also helped the client express her own anger and pain, which led to a discussion of her childhood experiences of a mother who had used her as an emotional crutch. The client described feeling at times like a dustbin where all the negative emotions were thrown.*

This particular client was helped to understand and experience her own troubling emotions. She gradually became able to distinguish between her own thoughts and feelings and those of others and learned when she was projecting onto others and when she was genuinely being empathic. This was established by the counsellor's being totally honest with the client and giving her accurate feedback when the client did pick up what the counsellor was thinking or feeling.

In this example we have a picture of one counsellor being overwhelmed by destructive counter-transference, while another more experienced counsellor was able to recognize the client's patterns and use her knowledge in order to help the client. Watkins (1983) describes five methods that the counsellor can utilize in order to manage any destructive counter-transference. These methods are: (a) self-analysis, (b) personal counselling, (c) supervision, (d) genuineness and self-disclosure, (e) referral.

Key practice point

It is important to recognize transference and counter-transference within the counselling relationship to avoid an irretrievable breakdown which may necessitate a referral. This necessitates honesty on the part of the counsellor and a willingness to work with sometimes powerful and disturbing emotions such as love, fear, grief, hate and anger.

Anticipating breakdown of the counselling relationship

Sometimes a referral needs to be made because of a personality clash between client and counsellor. Arnold Lazarus (1989) says that there does not have to be a mutual liking between counsellor and client for productive work to be done, although of course there needs to be respect and a willingness to engage in the counselling process. However, sometimes there may be such a clash of personality that even with supervision the counsellor can no longer continue with that particular client and it is in the interests of both client and counsellor that a referral is made. Similarly it may happen that there is a major clash of values between a counsellor and client and the counsellor finds it impossible to be 'non-judgemental' and will need to refer the client to another counsellor. However, Moira Walker (1993) argues that it is possible to work effectively with a client whose values the counsellor may find abhorrent.

There may occasionally be a mismatch in expectations of the client and counsellor. It is essential to ascertain what the client expects from counselling. If the client is wanting some practical advice and can only relate on this level and the counsellor is trying to explore the feeling level, then there may be a mutual bewilderment and loss of rapport. Some clients will feel more comfortable on a particular level, be it a practical action level, a thinking level or a feeling level. If the counsellor can acknowledge the client's preferred starting level and work with that, the client may then be able to explore his other levels in his own time (Hutchins, 1989). This could prevent a possible premature ending of counselling or the necessity of referral to a practitioner who can relate to the client's preferred way of working.

Key practice points

1 If there is a severe personality difference or value clash between client and counsellor a referral may be indicated.
2 It is necessary to monitor the client's expectations of counselling, such as being given practical advice, in order to determine whether or not counselling is the best option.

Referral from short-term to long-term counselling

Some counsellors wish to work in short-term counselling either because of their chosen clinical orientation (e.g. cognitive-analytic therapy, CAT) or because of the restrictions of the agency in which they work. This restriction in working is normally made clear to the client in, or even before, the first session. However, even though this way of working can be extremely effective and productive, there will be some clients who will need extra time. Sometimes the underlying problem only becomes clear after several sessions or it may be evident that the client has many problems that cannot be dealt with in the limited number of sessions available.

Here is a plea from a male colleague working in an agency that only permits a certain number of sessions.

> I am currently looking for a counsellor to refer one of my time-limited clients to. She'd like to continue with me but it's not allowed! She says she'd like someone who 'does it like you'. Words like 'eclectic' or 'person-centred' or whatever don't mean anything to her. I suspect it's more about finding the right personality fit. I telephoned someone – out of the BAC Directory – and I felt like a protective father trying to find someone good enough for my daughter. I was immediately put off by someone's gruff voice on the phone. I'm still looking. (What transference/counter-transference is here?) I've drafted a standard letter, which I'll be sending out to local counsellors, asking for their details for the purpose of referral from our time-limited services. It's surprising how many don't have any written material on themselves!

This account describes eloquently the concern or even anguish that can face a counsellor having to refer a client on because of agency limitations on the number of counselling sessions that are offered. Here is a situation where both client and counsellor wish to continue but are not allowed to do so. The counsellor's reluctance to refer is evident in his feeling 'like a protective father', while the client wants a counsellor who 'does it like you'. The counsellor who wrote the above account, because of this particular experience, decided to compile a dossier of local counsellors for referral purposes. He was surprised that some counsellors had no written material on themselves. This is certainly something that counsellors need both for their clients' information and for referrals. In addition an increasing number of nurses, teachers, personnel managers and others who use counselling skills in their work, have a need for clear information on counsellors to whom they can refer employees or colleagues.

The following account is by a counsellor who prefers to work with long-term clients.

Example   *This client had seen a counsellor for about six sessions. This counsellor had used some gestalt work with the client but seemingly had failed to establish trust with the client, as she had not felt safe enough to explore any issues in depth, and she was told by the counsellor, 'I cannot do any more for you.' The client found her own way to a new counsellor who was prepared to work in depth over a period of years. The client was seen once or twice a week over two years and was able to explore and come to terms with her sexual abuse, her suicidal impulses and her feelings of being utterly worthless.*

This counsellor was able to supply the respect, empathy and genuineness that the client needed over a sustained period of time. What is worrying is that the first counsellor not only failed to uncover any of the underlying factors involved in this client's problems but also failed to refer on to someone who was prepared to work on a long-term basis.

The following account is by a counsellor who normally works on a short-term contract but, instead of referring the client to someone else, decided to work herself with the client.

Example   *This client was referred to a counsellor on a short-term basis, but the counsellor quickly realized that the client had many problems which would not be resolved in the short time available. The counsellor needed to make a decision whether or not to refer this client to another coun-sellor who could give a long-term commitment. However, the counsellor was fascinated by the story emerging and decided to continue with the client. During a fraught three years during which the client presented with binge-eating, self-hatred, a history of sexual abuse, dependency, deep rage and spiritual deadness, the counsellor regretted many times the decision to stay with this client. However, the client gradually got in touch with her inner child (the hurt child and the joyful child that still are present within the adult – an idea originally from transactional analysis) and slowly learnt to forgive herself and accept the despised aspects of herself. The counsellor meanwhile had to dig deep within herself in order to hold this client and stay with her during a long process of testing by the client. With hindsight the counsellor would have referred this client to someone who was happier working on a long-term basis.*

Key practice points

1 Sometimes there are restrictions in the number of sessions that a counsellor can offer a client and there is a need to refer the client to someone who can work on a long-term contract.

2 This can cause problems if the client cannot afford private counselling and there are no facilities on offer. The counsellor may feel anger and sorrow that she has let the client down. The ending of the short-term contract could be problematic.

Referral because of geographical factors – counsellors' experiences of changing location

When a counsellor has to move location, there may be some loose ends for both client and counsellor. If the time factor is one of months, it may be possible to end most of the counselling contracts satisfactorily, the only possible sour note being that if the client wishes to see the counsellor again, this would probably not be possible. Unfortunately, there may be a few clients who need to be referred to another counsellor. This is especially likely if the move is made precipitously.

> ***Example*** *'When I knew I was going to move I found it quite difficult to tell certain clients in my private practice. Two or three in particular were quite affected or upset and even though I know two of them went on to counsellors I suggested for them, I felt that I had disrupted their progress. I kept in contact with one by telephone for a while, and he seemed to appreciate that.'*

In this account of a geographical move, the counsellor was very aware of some of his clients' feeling affected by the forced break in their counselling, and the use of the phrase 'I felt that I had disrupted their progress' indicates that he felt a responsibility for this. It seems that he had behaved responsibly towards his clients and had arranged other counselling for them and even used the phone as a contact for one of his clients. However, there is still the lingering concern for clients whose counselling has been interrupted.

Some counsellors feel not only responsible for interrupting the clients' progress but also sad themselves that they will not be able to continue with their clients. Cathy Siebold (1991) discusses her reluctance to tell her clients about her move and her 'sadness that I would not be able to see my patients through the therapeutic process to a mutually agreed on conclusion'. She also echoes the feeling of responsibility towards the clients when she states that 'therapists who leave must accept that they are breaking a bond that they encouraged to develop'. So counsellors may not only feel responsibility towards their clients and their future progression but also feel sadness at the premature endings and inability to continue towards a mutually satisfactory ending. The counsellor also has to cope with the feelings of clients who may accept the leaving with equanimity or with feelings of abandonment and betrayal.

Although most clients may reach a satisfactory ending within the time span or be settled with another counsellor, there may be a few clients for whom the counsellor's leaving may trigger off 'abandonment' feelings. This can be a tricky one to handle because of the counsellor's own feelings, which may include guilt. With the client's descent into despair, 'but you're the only one I can talk to', or 'everybody leaves me', the counsellor herself may feel despair or even anger because of all the practical and emotional pressures. This client needs careful handling with as much time as possible given to the emerging feelings while the referral is completed well before the counsellor's departure. Some therapists might welcome this situation because they would see the client's strong feelings as a 'break-through' with which to work. The departing counsellor needs to decide whether or not to encourage any communication, whether it be written or telephone, from the client. Some counsellors are able to maintain purposeful and therapeutic communication by telephone (Rosenfield, 1997).

Key practice point

If the counsellor leaves a place of work, there are terminations and referrals to consider, while also working through feelings of sadness and sometimes frustration at the forced departure.

Referral because of job change

When a counsellor changes her place of work, hopefully there is sufficient time to finish with the ongoing clients. The counsellor's feelings may range from sadness, especially if the change is involuntary, to elation if the new work is welcomed. There is the added dimension that, because the counsellor has probably not moved from the area, it may be possible for the clients to continue to see the counsellor on a private basis.

If the counselling work has not finished, the clients need to be referred to another counsellor. This can be hard for the client, the previous counsellor and the new counsellor. The client may express sadness and anger that the counselling work has not finished and may resist the efforts of the new counsellor. The original counsellor can prepare the client as much as possible by expressing regret at not finishing the work together, reviewing the work that has been done and sharing such information as is possible about the new counsellor. The new counsellor has the task of reassuring the client, who may be extremely sad and angry that the original counsellor has left, that the counselling work can continue.

The counsellor who is changing jobs will not only have to deal with the client's emotions, but their own sadness and possible anger. If the move is due to cut-backs there could be an increased frustration that the client may have to wait a long time to see another practitioner. There will most likely be a necessity to have increased supervision in order to contain both the client's feelings and the counsellor's feelings.

Depending on the rules of the counselling agency, it may be possible for clients to continue to see their counsellor on a private basis if the counsellor is available. This may be impossible for some clients because of financial problems. Some clients may welcome a private arrangement because the negotiated times could be more flexible.

Key practice points

1 When changing jobs there may be sadness and anger for both clients and counsellor if the work is unfinished.

2 Sometimes it is possible to negotiate a private arrangement with some clients so that the counselling work can continue with the same counsellor.

Taking on a client whose counsellor has become severely ill or who has died

You may be referred a client from a counsellor who can no longer work because of severe illness and, although this client is new to you, he or she will be in the middle of their counselling. Depending on the suddenness of the onset of the illness, the client may be in a crisis situation or may have worked through some of the feelings with the original counsellor. Ideally, you will be given some background information on the client. A period of time will need to be spent with the client, allowing him to express his feelings about the unfinished aspect of his counselling, before work can continue on his presenting problems. Some of the client's feelings of disappointment and anger may not have been expressed to the original counsellor for fear of upsetting her. The client may wish to write a letter to the original counsellor, which may or may not be sent, in order to fully express his feelings about the situation.

When a counsellor dies suddenly, the client may not only go through all the feelings of bereavement but there may be other issues involving loss that are triggered by this event. If the counsellor commits suicide or is murdered, everyone is likely to be in a state of shock. There may be a period of confusion while the client finds another counsellor unless the counsellor who has died has made provision for the clients by asking a colleague to look after her counselling clients in the event of her death. Probably the best that the colleague concerned can do is to see the clients in order to help them through the initial shock and to help them to find another counsellor. Meanwhile the colleague of the counsellor who has died may be having to deal with her own grief.

If you take on a client whose counsellor has died it will be necessary to deal with this crisis situation first. The death may trigger previous losses and past traumas for the client. The client may feel grief for the loss, or anger at all the unfinished business. If the client had been working through hostile feelings at the time, there may be guilt involved. The client may need to reveal deep feelings but is faced with a new counsellor. The client may have expectations of a counsellor built on his experiences of coun-selling before, and the new counsellor may need to explore the differences of counselling situations.

Example   *A counsellor saw a client whose original counsellor had died. The client was distraught and cried profusely
and said that she also wanted to die. There was no strong
suicidal intention, but the client felt abandoned and in pain
both physically and emotionally. The counsellor saw this
client three times in the first week, twice in the second and
third week and then the client felt strong enough to continue
weekly. It appeared that the client had formed a strong
attachment to her male counsellor and he was 'like a father
to me'. The client felt emotionally supported while she was
seeing her former counsellor, had managed to become more
independent after a difficult divorce and had found herself a
job. She had originally gone for counselling because of
depression. Now she felt abandoned, betrayed and frightened
that she would descend into a deep depression. The counsellor was warm and empathic and encouraged the client to
explore her feelings about the death of her counsellor. In the
first sessions the client expressed her grief and pain and then
began to talk about the feelings associated with abandonment. On exploration, the client was able to link these
feelings with how she had felt when her father left home
when she was eight years old. This was the first time she had
been able to experience how she had felt at that time. Before,
when she had remembered the experience, she had recalled
only a numbness. As she re-experienced and accepted these
earlier feelings, so the pain of her counsellor's death began to
recede and the fear of depression disappeared. The client
appeared brighter, began to smile again and was able to
explore the happy memories of her father and her gratitude
for her male counsellor's support. The client also felt grateful
to her new counsellor because she had not expected to be
able to trust a female counsellor enough to share her deepest
feelings, as she had always related to men rather than
women. The client was now able to see that this was because
she had been searching for a father figure.*

There are many implications for us as counsellors in contemplating our own death. It is necessary to make provisions for our
clients by asking a colleague to act in our clients' interests if we
should die unexpectedly. This means that a colleague should
know where we keep our client information and be prepared to

help the clients to find another counsellor if that is necessary. It is advisable to keep clear records of client details and which material needs to be disposed of, including written and taped client notes (Trayner and Clarkson, 1992).

Key practice points

1   If a counsellor dies, the clients may need much support before they can resume their normal counselling.
2   The death of a counsellor may trigger unexplored areas for the client.
3   Counsellors should prepare for the eventuality of their own death and ask a colleague to help the clients.

When the client should have been referred but wasn't

The majority of counsellors who answered the question 'Have you ever kept on working with a client who, with hindsight, it might have been better to refer elsewhere?' (Appendix 1, Question 8), responded in the affirmative. Why does a counsellor continue with a client when it is better to refer? Some counsellors find that the waiting lists for a specialist are long, especially in the NHS.

What about the personal reasons for continuing with a client when there should be a referral? How does one deal with the client saying 'You are the only one I can talk to' or the poignant 'Everyone gives up on me and everyone leaves me' or 'I thought that this time it would be different' or worse still 'If you refuse to see me I'll kill myself'?

Here is an example of a counsellor who responded to a plea from a client.

Example   A counsellor was leaving an agency and was preparing clients for her departure. One client reacted badly with the statement, 'Everyone gives up on me.' The counsellor did not wish to be yet another person who left her and suggested that the client see her privately. There were even arrangements made for reduced payment. The situation turned out well because the client then trusted the counsellor and was able to explore for the first time in depth the forces and circumstances behind the plea for help. This client was seen over a period of three years and was able to explore her abusive past and the reasons for her lack of self-esteem, and then was able to make a more satisfactory life for herself. She paid back in full not only the money that was due but also her counsellor's faith in her.

Here the counsellor responded personally to the plea made by the client, and the situation turned out well. The counsellor was in a position to offer private counselling to this client. Sometimes we are not in a position to do this. Sometimes a counsellor may not wish to offer private counselling, because it is possible that a client is being manipulative. Here is a discrepancy that sometimes occurs between giving a client an experience that they have never had, which is the warmth and caring that a counsellor may offer, and the fear some counsellors harbour that the client is a bottomless pit of need. I would put forward the suggestion that the latter fear is one that the counsellor would do well to explore in themselves. Sometimes our clients mirror our own experiences and fears, and by looking at these with self-analysis or with our own counsellor we can help both ourselves and our clients more effectively.

The following counsellor's account of a difficult experience of counselling is one that shows that sometimes it is better to refer the client rather than struggle with forces that can be attractive but destructive.

Example   *This client was an abuser in that she had a history of hurting children. The counsellor had already made the decision never to work with abusers, because of her own experience as a child in an abusive family. However, the counsellor found herself deeply moved by the inner workings and struggles of this client and responded readily to the client's pleas of 'Please don't refer me. Everyone else has always given up on me. I trust you. I've told you things that I've never told anyone else. It hurts so much when someone betrays me. I could never trust anyone else ever again.' Eventually, even the client realized how manipulative she was but she persisted with 'If you refer me I'll kill myself.' The counsellor found herself bound up in this manipulation, and* *realized that her own patterns from childhood were being activated. However, there was still the fascination of learning first-hand how an abuser's mind worked and, after all, wouldn't it be wonderful if this client could change? Perhaps, the counsellor reasoned, she could help this person, who was clearly unhappy, where she had been unable to help her own abusive mother, and perhaps M. Scott Peck was wrong to stress the difficulties or even impossibilities of counselling an 'evil' person (Peck, 1983)? During the three years of counselling that ensued the client made great progress with understanding herself and realizing that she viewed the world differently from most people. The counsellor regretted bitterly 'giving in' to the manipulation from the client, as it brought back feelings of resentment at being used by another person for their own needs and reactivated all the child abuse that 'had been dealt with'. The only satisfaction that the counsellor identified in not referring the client on, was the progress of the client and her gradual acceptance of herself and subsequent resolution of her difficulties. The counsellor felt that the personal price paid was too high, as her own relationships deteriorated under the pressure of reactivated memories. The counsellor felt that her original instinct not to work with an abuser had been the correct decision and this client should have been referred to someone else.*

Key practice point

Sometimes clients are not aware of their long-term needs of eventual independence and can manipulate the counsellor into continuing a problematic counselling relationship.

A client's positive experience of referral

The following is a client's account.

I saw this man for counselling. I did not feel happy. My problem was with men so how could seeing a man help? There would be these silences and it was embarrassing. I thought that he thought I was stupid. When he asked me if I would be happier seeing a woman, I jumped at the chance. 'Is that allowed?' He said he would see if there was a woman I could see but there might be a long wait. So I said yes. And it was a long wait, several months I think. But it was worth it because I knew she knew how I felt.

There was no embarrassing silence because I couldn't stop talking. And she listened and sometimes said something that helped me talk some more. It was good because she was not involved. I can't talk to my Mum because she always takes my side and my friends just tell me to leave my boyfriend. But when I talked and she just listened it was like I could hear myself and sort myself out. I didn't need to see her many times, things got better and I started to talk to my boyfriend and started to listen to him as well. I'm ever so glad I saw her and I would like to go back for counselling if I needed to. I tell all my friends but some of them don't understand.

This client's experience of referral was a positive one. Her male counsellor recognized that she was not comfortable with him and suggested the possibility of a female counsellor. He then arranged this for his client and the outcome was satisfactory.

A client's negative experience of referral

The following is a client's account.

My name is Isabel. This is one of two names that I was called as a child. I do not like either name.

I went to see a counsellor because I recognized that I had a tendency to become depressed, anxious and irritable on occasion with no great understanding as to the reason why I did so. My counsellor was gentle and understanding and used reflection and conflict resolution techniques to increase understanding and insights and release blocked energies. The only jarring note that struck me as a client was an intense reaction of feelings of rejection and abandonment as the uncertainty of whether or not the six-week contract would be extended. Upon negotiating an extension these very strong feelings subsided. The next shock was an unprecedented journey into hell upon probing into the emotions of sadness, loneliness and despair. I was thrown into the feelings of an abandoned child howling into nothingness. I felt that I was completely on my own with no-one there to help. I did not know how to ask for help. I withdrew into myself in order to run away from the confusion. When I saw my counsellor again she was calm and gentle and I regained stability. The next few sessions were of little significance as I attempted to recover from this unsettling episode.

After a summer gap of about six weeks, which I found difficult to cope with as I alternated between excited anticipation and apprehension, I saw my counsellor again. She suggested that as we appeared to have been travelling in circles and not getting anywhere, and as I appeared to have coped well over the summer, perhaps I would think of stopping counselling or seeing someone else. I was thrown back into the betrayed feelings of the small child – only this time it was intense fear. Also for the first time I began to receive images of oral sexual abuse at an early age and images of attempted suffocation with a pillow. When I asked for help from my counsellor she was there for me, we discussed the memories, she helped me comfort the distressed inner child, and was immensely supportive and caring. She told me that she had similar events in her own past. Was this the breakthrough? In a sense it was because for the first time I had trusted someone enough to share events that had been completely suppressed and for the first time I cried.

However, now things began to go badly wrong. I started to probe more deeply in order to understand more about these long-suppressed events. The new material that emerged (including maternal sexual abuse, physical abuse and neglect) struck at the very core of my being, at my shaky self-esteem, at my belief in myself. I could not speak about this. I felt dizzy and nauseous. I did not want to eat. I was not sleeping much and when I did I had terrifying nightmares. My counsellor was perplexed, troubled and angry, and again talked of me seeing someone else. She told me she felt incompetent to deal with me. I went into some kind of shock and instead of releasing blocks this manoeuvre produced intense incapacitating pain. I attempted to discuss what was happening at the next session but it appears that my distress had triggered off a reaction in her and she stated that she could no longer deal with me as a client. She agreed to see me one more time but cancelled this session by phone and letter.

I would hope that you can imagine my feelings at this time. Long-suppressed memories of sexual abuse, attempted infanticide and neglect had emerged, with the accompanying emotions of a frightened, lonely child. These memories and feelings I had shared for the first time with someone who appeared to understand, accept and support me. When memories emerged that threatened my very core image, when thoughts of suicide flitted through my mind, when forbidden anger tentatively, warily emerged – my support crumbled. For whatever personal reasons my counsellor withdrew from me at the most critical time. I was left with the most intense physical chest pain I have ever experienced, overwhelming sadness and sense of loss, feelings of betrayal, abandonment, rejection, anger, and worst of all for a trainee counsellor, an intense fear at the thought of ever being a client again.

I have tried to see other therapists. I can only talk to someone I know cannot be a long-term therapist. I cannot place myself in the hands of someone long enough to form the trusting relationship that is necessary to explore the issues I have to face. I did trust someone and that resulted in unbearable pain.

I am now faced with an intolerable dilemma. I know that in order to be an effective, and safe, counsellor I have to deal with my own issues but I dare not allow myself to be in the position of being hurt so much again.

So, Counsellor, look into your own mental process, your own emotions, your own motivations, before you 'help' another person. Perhaps you may come across a client who is more sensitive that you, more empathic, more delicate, and easily crushed under the weight of your personal problems. *It is not enough to think that trust, hard won, can be transferred to another counsellor like a parcel. At the very least, a referral situation should be thoroughly discussed with your client so that she or he does not feel rejected and cast aside like unwanted rubbish.*

I feel privileged that Isabel has allowed me to use her story. I feel angry for her. There are many issues that arise for us as counsellors in such circumstances.

Isabel's account of her painful experiences of 'referral' accentuate the need for counsellors to have dealt substantially with their own past traumas to prevent such interference in the counselling situation. There are varying views on how much personal counselling is necessary, with the psychodynamic school seeing lengthy personal therapy as absolutely essential, and some of the cognitive-behavioural schools not believing that it is necessary in order to practise as a counsellor. Lazarus believes that it is not necessary to have undergone therapy in order to be a therapist (Lazarus, 1989). Most training counselling establishments now suggest or demand that the students undergo a minimum number of individual personal counselling sessions as well as sometimes attending a personal development group. The Thameslink/UEL Counselling Diploma course, for example, demands attendance at a Personal Development Group for thirty-six weeks in the first year, and a minimum number of sessions of personal counselling for each student. Sometimes it becomes obvious to both trainee and tutor that the trainee needs more personal counselling sessions in order to work through her personal difficulties. Of course many trainees have entered upon the course because they have already worked through some of their personal difficulties and found counselling to have helped them so much that they wish to become counsellors themselves. From October 1998 all counsellors who wish to be accreditated by the British Association for Counselling must have had a minimum of forty hours of personal counselling.

Another important issue that arises from Isabel's account is the need to thoroughly discuss the referral with the client. All counsellors have their limitations and, if a counsellor finds herself in a situation that she cannot handle, she is ethically bound to refer to another counsellor after discussion with her supervisor. However, if Isabel's counsellor had handled this referral properly, a lot of the pain would have been avoided. Apparently, this counsellor wrote a list of names down in the letter that stated she did not wish to see Isabel again. There was no attempt to ease Isabel into the new counselling situation and no follow-up. It appears that this counsellor was too bound up in her own affairs to bother about her client.

It sounds as if Isabel could have made a complaint to BAC about this counsellor's behaviour. However, Isabel felt that what had happened was all her fault, and it was several years before she saw the situation clearly.

Isabel is now a practising counsellor and is very caring of her clients. She says that she sometimes worries about clients too much and becomes exhausted if she is not careful. She is learning to trust herself but is still nervous about older women in authority.

Competent handling of a referral to another counsellor

If it is decided by the counsellor upon careful consideration and exploration with the counselling supervisor that it is in the interests of the client that a referral be made, then it is crucial that the whole procedure is handled sensitively. The client should be put in the picture and be given some choice. The counsellor may need to contact the other counsellor to find out if the referral is possible and then the client asked if they wish any information to be passed to this counsellor. The counsellor may make the referral, or the client may prefer to initiate contact himself.

A helpful way to facilitate a referral to another counsellor is to review with the client what has happened during counselling and how far the client has progressed. Sometimes the benefits of the counselling can be lost when a referral is made and the client does not celebrate the movement and change that has already taken place. The client may then appreciate the idea of counselling being seen as a journey, with one particular counsellor going only so far with him while another counsellor may be able to go further along the road. In this way some of the feelings involved in the change of counsellors can be explored and the counsellor may be able to share her feelings of sadness at not being able to continue with this client, but also feelings of satisfaction at the progress already made.

Some counsellors may wish to have an update of progress of a referred client. This could come from the client, who may ask if he can write to the original counsellor. The client may wish to let the original counsellor know how he is, and he may feel pleased that the counsellor is genuinely interested in his progress. The counsellor can choose whether to reply or not. There could, however, be an interference in the new counselling relationship if the client believed that he was still receiving counselling, albeit by letter, from the original counsellor. A progress report may come from the new counsellor if she is asked to produce one and is willing to do so with the client's permission.

Unhelpful reasons for not referring the client on

It is useful to consider some of the possible obstacles to clear thinking that may prevent us referring a client to another professional.

1   I'm in private practice and I need the money.
2   I need the experience of working with this particular problem that the client presents.
3   I don't know anyone in my area to refer to.
4   I like, or am fascinated by, this client and do not wish him to see someone else.
5   I need to be liked by my clients and, if I refer my clients to someone else, they will not like me.
6   I feel a failure if I refer clients.
7   I am afraid that the client will be angry with me.
8   I was trained and supervised in a way that rarely if ever regarded referral as legitimate.

Referral checklist for counsellors and supervisors

1 What leads you to believe that you have the necessary training, skills and competency to work with and not refer particular clients?

2 To what extent do you subscribe to the view that clients deserve the best available source of help, even if this is not necessarily yours, and even if this entails your putting work into helping someone find other services?

3 How can you balance your need for extended experience (by sometimes taking on a client whose problems are outside your training and experience) against the client's right to know about the limits of your competency and about alternative services?

4 What evidence do you seek, and rely on, to demonstrate that the theoretical orientation in your training is capable of safely, economically and effectively addressing a wide rage of pre-senting problems?

5 Is there a point in the therapeutic relationship beyond which you would not refer a client on, or suggest referral, even when a need for more appropriate help might be indicated, because the disruption itself might be damaging?

6 What sort of contract might you agree with a client who wants to see you but who is on a long waiting list for a specialist and/or free therapy service?

Summary

1 If the counsellor is aware of strong feelings from the client that seem to be excessive in the situation, this awareness can be used to explore the client's problems rather than necessitating a referral.

2 When the counsellor is aware of his or her own particularly strong feelings in the counselling situation, this may indicate feelings that the client has difficulty recognizing or dealing with, or the feelings may belong to the counsellor. The coun-sellor may need to work through her own issues, and/or may need to refer the client on.

3 A personality clash or major difference in values may necessi-tate a referral.

4   Some clients may need more sessions than the counsellor, working for a particular organization, may be able to offer, and may need to be referred for more counselling.

5   An ending may occur with a particular counsellor because of an unexpected move or job change for either client or counsellor.

6   A referral may be handled by reviewing the client's progress and discussing options. The client may prefer to personally make contact with the new counsellor if this is possible. If the original counsellor refers the client, with the client's permission some information may be exchanged. The original counsellor may wish to ask for a progress report from the new counsellor, with the client's permission.

6

Problems and Considerations in the Ending Phase

This chapter explores problematic endings when the counselling ends abruptly or the counsellor or the client is reluctant to end. Sometimes the ending is contracted and final and sometimes it is not necessarily final, if the counsellor operates an 'open-door' policy for clients to return if they wish.

Abrupt ending by client

Termination can be abrupt. Although the counsellor may prefer to have at least one session of review before the client leaves, sometimes a client simply does not arrive for an appointment. If possible, the client should be contacted either by phone or letter and offered another appointment. A phone call can be a more personal contact and more likely to achieve a result. Some counsellors, however, believe that a phone call is intrusive, and some clients may not wish to be contacted in this way. A clear initial contract regarding missed appointments should be made, so that both client and counsellor are aware of the procedure that should be followed. In private practice this may mean that the client is expected to pay for missed appointments but also has fixed times already allocated for the next appointments. In certain organizations it may be that the client is expected to phone if he cannot make the appointment.

The client may turn up for the next appointment with profuse apologies. However, if the client does not offer a satisfactory explanation, it may indicate either some resistance to what is happening in the counselling process or that the possibility of working through an ending phase should be discussed. Either way, this could be used as an opportunity to review the progress of the counselling.

It is sometimes the case when contacting a client by phone that an ending is negotiated there and then. This can leave the counsellor feeling unsatisfied, although the client may feel fine.

> **Example**   *A counsellor had to phone a client because she needed to change the appointment time, and this was an appointment that had been sent after the client had not turned up. The client was slightly bemused because she had not registered that she had an appointment and explained rather sheepishly that she felt much better and really did not need any more sessions. The counsellor felt relieved for her but also annoyed that she had not bothered to notify anyone.*

It is possible that some clients may regard seeing a counsellor rather like seeing a doctor, especially in GP surgeries, in that when the client feels better they not only 'forget' to turn up to appointments but also 'forget' to let the counsellor know. Some clients may genuinely not possess the social skills required to use the telephone in order to cancel appointments, or may not be assertive enough to let the counsellor know that they no longer require counselling. I have occasionally come across clients who had difficulties with authority figures, and who genuinely could not attend for a session, forgot to let me know, and then were afraid that I would be angry with them. This would be an issue to be addressed if the client returned for the next session.

If the client is sent a letter offering another appointment and then does not turn up for the second time, the counsellor again has to decide whether or not to pursue the matter. Some counsellors will adopt the attitude that clients have to take full responsibility for the keeping of appointments and for letting the counsellor know if they cannot attend, and this could be discussed with the client at the initial interview. However, the counsellor can be left wondering how the client is or if, as a counsellor, she 'said something wrong'. This can be an unpleasant feeling.

Example   *A counsellor recalled looking up the client's notes in the GP surgery in which she was working when a client did not arrive for an appointment. The client had been very unhappy about continuing with a third pregnancy, and the counsellor felt relieved to see a note to the effect that the counselling session had helped her feel better about having the baby.*

One of the problems of working in a GP surgery or in student counselling is that clients may wish to 'drop-in' when they want to and 'drop-out' again just as quickly. Garfield (1989) mentions advising counselling students to go over notes and tapes to see if they had missed possible indicators of premature ending by the client, but he does not think that this will significantly reduce future drop-out rates. Some interesting research was conducted by Shapiro (1974), who found a correlation between clients who dropped out of therapy and the negative views that the therapist had about their progress in treatment. Shapiro cautions trainee therapists and their supervisors to be more aware of their affective reactions to clients and the possible consequences of negative counter-transference.

In the questionnaire given to some practising counsellors, the question about the feelings of the counsellor after an abrupt ending (Appendix 1, Question 16) produced an interesting variety of answers. Some counsellors felt a sense of failure and questioned themselves as to what had gone wrong. Some felt a sense of rejection, anxiety, sadness and concern. There was surprise for some counsellors and even relief and pleasure for others. Trainee counsellors in particular seemed to feel especially vulnerable when a client ended abruptly, and they questioned and blamed themselves. Experience in counselling helps one to realize that all clients progress at their own pace, and whilst some clients need a structure of counselling sessions over a specified period of time, other clients may make good use of one or two sessions and achieve all they wish from this short time (Talmon, 1990).

Example   *A client came suffering from depression. She described everything as being too much trouble and said that everything seemed overwhelmingly difficult. The counsellor* *was quite concerned about her because she sometimes appeared to go into a trance-like state and she was finding it difficult to focus her thoughts. It appeared that she felt pulled in different directions by her family and was trying to please everyone and finding it impossible. The counsellor helped her to explore what was most important for her in this situation and to begin to look at different ways of handling the people around her. The counsellor fully expected to see her for several sessions. However, she turned up at the next session looking completely different, sounding bright and chirpy, and informed the counsellor that she felt wonderful, like her old self, and now able to cope well with everything! Apparently she had very nearly not come at all, but her partner had told her to come and explain how well she felt.*

In this example the counsellor was grateful that the client had bothered to come, because, if she had not done so, the counsellor might have been left wondering what had gone wrong and how she was. Although the counsellor appreciated that the client felt that she was back to normal, she was advised to see her doctor who had known her for a long time, and it was emphasized that she could have some more counselling if she felt that she needed it at any time. There are times when it is difficult to believe in such rapid recovery.

It is important to discuss the particular arrangements for counselling sessions with clients as early as possible, so that the clients are aware of procedures regarding missed appointments. Individual counsellors may have different ideas about non-attendance. Some counsellors may have contracted with the client a certain number of sessions which are expected to be paid for irrespective of attendance and sometimes in advance. In other circumstances the client does not pay but may need to be aware that his place may be taken because of the pressure of waiting lists. I remember someone asking me why he had not received another appointment from his counsellor when he had cancelled via a receptionist, and it was obvious that the counsellor concerned had not explained the appointment procedure, which in this case was that another appointment had to be requested or it was assumed that the client no longer wished to attend. It is also important to be aware that some clients may have difficulty using the telephone and may be happier writing a note.

Key practice questions

1 What feelings come up for you when a client ends abruptly?
2 Was it clear to the client that you wished to be notified if the client no longer wanted to attend?
3 Was it clear to the client how to change an appointment? Was there a problem using the telephone?
4 Is it permissible to phone the client at home or work?
5 If the client cancelled, was it clear that he would, or would not, be sent another appointment?
6 How did you feel towards the client and his progress in counselling?

Premature ending by client

Another ending of counselling which may feel right for the client but can leave the counsellor with mixed feelings is when the client indicates a wish to end unilaterally. The client may genuinely think that the problem he came with in the first place has either been resolved or at least substantially addressed and that there is no further reason for attending sessions. However, the counsellor may be concerned about ending because of other issues that have arisen during the counselling process. It often feels frustrating for a counsellor to be left thinking that there is 'unfinished business'.

> ***Example*** *A client came to counselling with acute anxiety about his sexuality and sexual identity. He was not sure whether he felt male or female, heterosexual or homosexual. During the process of counselling he realized that, although he had had homosexual experiences, his main attraction was towards women. This left him with the option of staying male and being sexual towards women or trying to become female, using hormones and surgery, while retaining an attraction towards women. He in fact managed to overcome his fear of his 'masculinity' and even established a loving relationship with a woman and her children. At this point the client wished to end the counselling sessions. The counsellor was left feeling uneasy because she felt that his integration had taken place very quickly and that, if anything were to go wrong, he seemed to have few coping resources. However, the sessions were ended with the proviso that if the*

client needed more counselling in the future he could contact the counsellor again. The crisis came three months later when the counsellor was on holiday. Fortunately, provisions had been made for a colleague to see emergencies. When the counsellor saw the client again she discovered that his relationship had broken up because the woman had returned to her husband. The client needed to work through his grief for his loss and his intense anger against the husband. After several months during which he learned to accept the aggressive feelings in himself that had frightened him previously, he established a relationship with a younger, unmarried woman and appeared to be much more stable and integrated.

Most of the counsellors who answered Question 14 in the questionnaire (Appendix 1) offered an 'open door' for future counselling sessions. If the client knows that he can contact the counsellor in the future it may happen that the client will partake of further counselling when he feels the need to. This can feel very satisfying for the counsellor because, not only has the instinctive feeling that there was further work to be done been vindicated, but there is the knowledge that the client may be better able to cope after further counselling sessions. This practice is recommended by Cummings and Sayana (1995) on the grounds that the psychotherapist could be seen as a 'psychological family practitioner', with the client returning at various points over the life cycle.

> **Key practice point**
>
> Counselling can be seen as a life-long process and the counsellor as a resource available throughout the client's life cycle, and delivered accordingly.

Breaks from counselling experienced by the client as endings

Occasionally, the client may decide to terminate the counselling sessions when the counsellor is on holiday or there is a break in counselling for some other reason, such as illness or academic terms. This may indicate that the client had been contemplating an ending but had not wanted to broach the subject to the counsellor. It may be that the client realized that he could cope well without counselling and so decided to finish, but had not, however, identified lack of assertiveness as a problem area. If at all possible the client should be invited back for at least one session in order to review progress and make an ending if that is what the client wishes to do.

Sometimes the true situation is that the client feels abandoned by the counsellor and is feeling hurt and angry. This indicates that there is more work to be done and the break has precipitated memories of past occasions when the client felt abandoned. The reason why the client has not returned to counselling after the break may be that the feelings have been very powerful and bewildering. The client's 'adult' self may be telling him that it is only a temporary break, while the client's 'child' self is in distress. An invitation by the counsellor to return for more counselling may be needed for the client to be able to understand what is happening and to be able to tackle these strong feelings.

Key practice points

1 Breaks from counselling may be used by the client as a way of ending the counselling.
2 Breaks from counselling may produce strong feelings for the client indicating further work to be done.

Introducing the subject of termination – how long should the termination process take?

The termination process may take place in one session. The counselling may have naturally come to a review session, and the client may spontaneously suggest that it is the right time to end. This may feel satisfactory to both client and counsellor. Some writers stress that counselling should not be terminated during the session in which the idea of ending is first verbalized (Ward, 1984). In practice it often happens. However, sometimes the counsellor may feel that there are more issues to be explored. The client's wishes are to be respected at all times but the counsellor may feel the need to invite the client to contact him for more counselling sessions in the future. Sometimes the client does indeed contact the counsellor and is able to progress further.

One way of discovering how the client feels about the ending of counselling is to initiate the topic and have a review session. The counsellor can facilitate the client in exploring how he has benefited from counselling, how far he has come, and what other issues he needs to explore. This is a useful exercise to clarify why the client came in the first place and how he has changed. Of course, if there has been little movement it is also useful to ask the client whether he feels that counselling is helping and if there is an alternative for him. A review can often focus the client, and a planned ending process can often begin. This may entail a few more sessions and then a follow-up session. Lamb (1985) describes a seven-session time-frame model of termination in which session one is a termination plan, sessions two and three review old and unfinished business, sessions four and five look at the therapeutic relationship, session six explores future plans, and session seven is leave-taking and discussion of any further contact. Lamb does allow for flexibility in this model in that stages of termination could be considered rather than specific time frames.

Some clients may feel a panic reaction to the idea of termination. This is probably an indication of deeper issues that can be explored further. There may be a fear of abandonment that can reach back into early childhood or infancy and which was perhaps triggered when the idea of endings was broached. Some psychoanalytic or psychodynamic schools of therapy believe that up to a third of the time spent in therapy should be devoted to the ending. After the client has been given the opportunity to explore his difficulties with endings, he may need a structured approach to termination, with weekly appointments giving way to fortnightly appointments, then monthly appointments until he feels confident that he has not been abandoned unceremoniously.

***Example** A client who was abandoned by his schizophrenic mother and spent most of his childhood in a children's home indicated strongly that he did not wish to end abruptly, because it would be too painful for him. He needed a long process of gradually letting go, being able to 'check-in' with his progress at monthly intervals over a period of a year. He consolidated the work that had been accomplished in* *counselling and gradually began to trust himself and his progress. The last sessions were mostly devoted to acknowledging and celebrating the hard work he had put in over the years in understanding, accepting and finally being able to love himself.*

Key practice points

1 The termination process may be completed in one session.
2 The termination process may trigger issues of rejection and abandonment for the client and so more time may be needed to deal with these emerging feelings.

Termination in time-limited work

Sometimes a client may only attend counselling for one session. If this is not planned, the counsellor may be left wondering if she has not met the client's needs sufficiently. However, the client may have found that one session where he has been listened to with attention, and non-judgementally, has been enough to make significant changes (Feltham, 1997). Talmon (1990) found that seventy-eight per cent of his clients stated that they had significantly improved as a result of receiving one counselling session. Single session therapy (SST) can be planned in advance for those clients who have specific problems that will respond to focused solution-based interventions. Some counsellors regard every session as a counselling unit in itself (Mahrer, 1988, and family therapists, Boscolo and Bertrando, 1993).

Another short-term model, the two-plus-one model, was developed in order to deal with NHS waiting lists. The client would be seen for two sessions and then have a follow-up session after a month (Barkham, 1989).

In all strictly time-limited counselling the termination process is built into the counselling from the beginning. Because the sessions are limited, both counsellor and client know when the ending will happen, and this focuses the work. Garfield (1989: 118) states that there can be a positive motivational effect when 'both participants in therapy know they have a specifed and limited amount of time in which to try and secure some type of postive outcome'. Of course even in time-limited counselling some clients may terminate earlier than expected.

Wilson (1996) discusses different forms of contracting a fixed number of sessions with a clear termination point. There is the 'holding' arrangement for one to three sessions, the 'mini-commitment' for four to six sessions, the 'time-focused' for ten to thirteen sessions, the 'time-extended' for twelve-plus sessions with four sessions' notice of finishing, and the 'time-expanded' with two months' notice of finishing. The termination procedure would include discussion with the client about the future and any referral that might take place.

Key practice point

Time-limited counselling may involve one planned session, two sessions with a follow-up session, or a specified number of sessions with a planned finishing date. This approach to counselling termination will help to focus the work.

Dealing with resistance to termination – dependent clients

Termination may become problematic if the client shows a dependent personality orientation. This dependency is associated with certain traits such as desire for help and support from others, compliance with rules and authorities, and sensitivity to interpersonal cues (Bornstein, 1993). While a dependent client may appear co-operative and eager to please the counsellor, some of the desires involved, such as wanting to stay under the counsellor's care and protection, can interfere with the counselling process and the aim of autonomy.

This kind of client may find it very difficult to become independent and assertive, and this can obviously interfere with the termination process. The counsellor may find that she wishes to 'mother' the client and at first may feel protective, but then she finds that she becomes irritated with the lack of progress being made. Bornstein (1993) recommends that the positive aspects of the counselling work are emphasized while some feedback is given on how the client's dependency needs may affect relationships. It is interesting to explore where this dependency originates from, and this will probably vary from client to client.

This poem, written by a client, illustrates the intense yearning for closeness but also the intense fear of abandonment.

. . . I become lost in the world of gentle, loving touch
And yet I yearn for it.
Caring leads to greater pain
When inevitable abandonment occurs.
If there is indifference then
Rejection is meaningless.
If there is hatred then
Parting brings relief.
But where there is tenderness
Parting can only be painful.

Example   *A client had a mother who physically abused her and rarely showed her any love or positive affirmation. The father was not often at home, because he was a lorry driver, and left the care of the children in his wife's hands. The child showed a pattern of intense attachment to any female, such as a teacher or care worker, and then an incident would occur where the child would feel betrayed and not contact this person again. This pattern continued into adult life, where friendships would be formed only to be broken when the client felt she had been slighted or ignored or betrayed. Her relationships with men were intense and short-lived.*

This client seemed eager to please and 'do the right things'. Little presents appeared because 'you are good to me'. The counsellor felt both protective and uneasy as though walking on egg shells. The client had very low self-esteem and did not like herself despite spending a lot of money on herself and always appearing well-dressed and made-up. There was much hard work with building the client's self-esteem and releasing the anger that had been festering inside for many years. Very slowly this client began to let go of her childhood and her desire for her mother's approval, found herself a job and a regular boyfriend, and gradually began to give herself the positive affirmation that she had wanted all her life. As the client's life improved, so termination of the counselling seemed to be indicated, but the client's dependency seemed to reappear and she appeared to slip back emotionally. Several sessions were devoted to reinforcing the gains made, with much positive affirmation of the progress, and eventually the client herself decided that she was ready to leave.

This example illustrates that sometimes 'symptoms often reappear during the termination phase' (Kupers, 1988: 36). The client may become extremely distressed, thinking that he is 'back to square one', but with reassurance and an emphasis on the gains made the client will usually emerge intact.

It is thought by some counsellors that some forms of counselling, such as brief counselling, cognitive-behavioural counselling, the Egan approach, and person-centred counselling, for different reasons do not necessarily foster any dependence issues for the client. Time-limited counselling has the notion of termination clear from the beginning, with a set number of sessions leading to a final review of progress made. Cognitive-behavioural counselling and Egan's 'Skilled Helper' approach emphasize problem management with cognitive analysis and action planning by the client. Carl Rogers believed that the person-centred approach, with the counsellor being consistently genuine, would not foster dependency problems. Rogers (1951: 201) states that 'in client-centred therapy . . . this involved and persistent dependence transference relationship does not tend to develop'. However, perhaps person-centred counsellors under-play the 'seductive-ness' of the warmth and empathy that is also a vital part of the approach and which may never before have been experienced by the client. A therapeutic approach that uses the relationship between the counsellor and the client as the most important element inherently runs the risk of creating termination problems.

However true the claims of brief counsellors and person-centred counsellors that there is no problem with dependency issues, there may well be a problem with long-term counselling. Kupers (1988: 71) acknowledges that 'longer therapies that probe for deeper-lying conflicts tend to foster more dependency, resulting in heightened termination issues'. Freud apparently had problems himself with dependency issues, because he had a fear of becoming dependent on others, to the extent that he undertook his own analysis and was afraid of old age because of his possible dependence on others (Kupers, 1988). Although Freud conceived some good theories on termination (Freud, 1937), his fear of dependency resulted in difficulties with ending relationships with colleagues and clients. Freud had problems with helping his clients examine their feelings about the ending of therapy and the loss of their analyst. Therapists and counsellors now, following theorists such as Bowlby, are becoming more aware of the necessity of allowing the client to freely explore the issues of loss.

Another interesting way of looking at the problem of the dependent client is for the counsellor to explore within herself for any signs of encouraging such dependency. If a client seems excessively dependent on the counsellor it may be that the client is actually responding to the counsellor's needs. This can happen, say Mearns and Thorne (1988: 134), even in the person-centred approach and indicates an abuse of power behind 'the creation of excessive dependency'. If the counsellor were to examine the situation carefully it may be that she would find that she needs to be needed, or is reluctant to negotiate boundaries or endings 'for fear of hurting the client' and thereby denying the client respon-sibility for his own process.

Example   *A counsellor recounted a story of when she was herself in counselling and found herself becoming very dependent on the counsellor. The client thought about the counsellor all the time and was always wondering what the counsellor would think or say about whatever was happening in the client's life. Whenever something happened the client would want to ring up the counsellor and tell her. The client lived for the weekly meetings and would feel 'high' for a day afterwards. It felt like an addiction. The client began to feel uneasy about the situation, and put forward the possibility that there could be a break in the counselling. The counsellor appeared reluctant to consider this possibility and insisted that the client needed to continue in order to work through what was happening. The client began experiencing fear when the counselling session was due and, where before there had only been a feeling of excitement before a session, now there was anticipation and anxiety. After a few sessions of this the client decided to terminate the counselling against the advice of the counsellor. Although there was a feeling of loss the client gradually began to feel more at ease with herself, less and less drawn back towards the counsellor and more able to begin to understand what had been going on. She believed that she had been drawn into the counsellor's needs and her dependency was a result of this. Once the connection was broken the client no longer felt the need to be dependent and*

*indeed felt very angry with the counsellor. She decided not to
pursue the matter further because she did not wish to contact
this counsellor ever again.*

Key practice points and question

1   Emphasize the positive aspects of the counselling experience when
dealing with a dependent client.
2   Explore the difficulties that can be experienced in a counselling
relationship when the client is dependent.
3   If you have many dependent clients are you in some way encouraging this dependency?

Ending experienced as a bereavement by the client

Ending a counselling relationship may feel like a bereavement to
clients. The therapeutic relationship may have been experienced
as positive and rewarding for the client, and the counsellor may
sometimes be unaware of the depth of the mourning process
that the client undergoes. As one of Kupers's clients admits, 'Just
when you've become an important part of my life, you're saying
it's time to stop and say goodbye' (Kupers, 1988: 2). Not every
client needs to go through an emotional termination process but
some may have formed a deep attachment to the counsellor. A
problem may arise when both the counsellor and the client are
unaware of the depth of the client's feelings and the client is hit
by an intense reaction later.

The client may have intellectualized the necessity of the ending
of the therapeutic bond. He may have examined the problems
that led him into counselling, appreciated working these through
and seen the results in the way he feels, thinks and acts.
However, the attachment to the counsellor may have run deeper
than is realized, and if this is the case then the client may go
through a mourning period after the counselling has ended.

Each individual mourns in his own particular fashion. The client
may find himself experiencing such feelings as numbness, denial,
anger, panic, physical distress, guilt, depression. Numbness pro-
tects us from the overwhelming feelings of grief. Denial and
disbelief make us dwell in the past. Anger helps us to express
frustrations. Panic sometimes brings muscle tensions, confusion
and helplessness. Our physical body may feel battered with pain,

nausea, and stress symptoms. There may be extreme tiredness. Guilt may be present – 'Perhaps she decided to end the counselling because I said such and such . . . or I did such and such . . . or I expressed anger . . .'. Depression may descend because of the feelings of emptiness and loneliness.

Example *A client wrote this poem after her counselling had ended abruptly and she suffered a grief reaction.*

> *You have dissipated into fragile memory.*
> *I thought I had you firmly grasped*
> *But once again you slipped into a deceptive mirage.*
> *I have entered, yet again, the eternity of darkness*
> *Where there is no hope of relief.*
> *Even the thought of death, once comforting, is now daunting*
> *In its finality.*
> *I don't even care what is the truth anymore.*
> *I live on in apathy.*
> *The miracle of life parades in front of unseeing eyes.*
> *What was important, now has no meaning.*
> *What was found has been lost.*
> *The senses shrivel.*
> *Black cords strangle the light within*
> *Slowly and painfully*
> *Until all hope has been squashed*
> *And all love has been extinguished.*

This particular client unfortunately suffered an unexpectedly severe grief reaction when her counselling ended, and she felt unable to express this until her pain had diminished, she wrote this poem, and talked extensively to a friend. When she was better able to understand her reaction, she realized that her counselling had enabled her to withstand the grief of loss, and eventually to express her feelings and not descend into deep depression that had been her wont before her counselling sessions.

One hopes that the counselling process itself has given the client some understanding or techniques to deal with his mourning process. The client will have learned the importance of acceptance and expression of feelings. 'Sorrow, like the river, must be given vent lest it erode its bank' (Grollman, 1987: 61). Ironically, if he could express his feelings directly to his counsellor, he would not be undergoing the mourning process. If the counsellor operates an 'open-door' policy, and the client were to feel extreme loss after counselling had ended, the client may be able to express some of his feelings and understand what had precipitated them. A sad state of affairs could arise when a client goes to another counsellor in order to express his feelings about his loss and then forms another attachment and so repeats the whole pattern. In this situation the counsellor would need to give enough time for the client to work through his repeating pattern of loss, which may have arisen from early childhood. The ending process may need to be staggered so that the client can 'check-in' at gradually lengthening intervals until the pattern of extreme loss and feelings of abandonment is broken and he feels strong enough to continue on his own.

> **Example**   *A client presented with many problems, including relationship difficulties. He had never had a long relationship with a woman because as soon as he began to relax and think that this was 'the one', he would start to see the woman as evil and ugly. It transpired that this client's mother could not cope with a child and so left him in a children's home, would visit infrequently and sometimes not arrive when she said she would. As a result the boy closed off part of himself and concentrated on surviving. He found socializing to be extremely difficult and relationships almost impossible because of the low opinion he had of himself. Through immense hard work on himself he found a job and began to make friends. In counselling he gradually got in touch with the hurt child within and began to feel stronger and more at ease with himself. After two years the ending process was staggered, with weekly meetings going to fortnightly meetings, then monthly sessions, and then 'check-in' sessions at two- to three-month intervals because of his heightened sensitivity to loss (particularly of a female carer).*

If a client is able to decide himself on the ending time then it would probably be rarer for a prolonged mourning process to occur. In person-centred counselling 'the client dictates the endpoint' (Mearns and Thorne, 1988: 144). If the counsellor has an 'open-door' policy then the client might return to the counsellor in order to look at the underlying reasons for such a strong reaction.

It may not be possible for a counsellor to let the client dictate the ending time, nor operate an open-door policy, and if this is so then some sort of concrete termination process needs to be considered even in short-term counselling. A client can sometimes form a deep attachment to a counsellor within a very short period of time. This may be because the counsellor is showing a caring and listening attitude at possibly the worst period of the client's life. Also some clients have never before experienced a non-judgemental and empathic relationship of any kind. The counsellor needs to recognize this possibility because, not only may the client go through a very painful grief process, but there is also the chance that, because of the hurt the client experiences, he may denigrate the benefits that counselling has given him.

Another kind of bereavement that the client may suffer is the loss of his 'old self'. In the process of counselling, many changes can take place; the client may have lost old assumptions and ways of thinking, feeling and behaving, and this may feel like a death of the old self. Most clients are only too happy to find their 'real self', or aspects of it, and feel only relief that the 'old self' is dead. Other clients may realize that under stressful conditions this 'old self' tends to resurrect itself but this is often a temporary situation. However, some clients may actually need to mourn their 'old self'. Mearns states that 'the client at the end of a successful counselling process will have lost a lot' (Mearns, 1993: 38).

Key practice point

Consider the value of gradually tailing off the counselling sessions, offering 'booster' sessions, or operating an open-door policy for clients in order to maintain the gains made during the counselling process and mitigate the loss of the relationship that may be experienced by the client.

'Too-easy' termination

There is a school of thought suggesting that a client may show a 'flight into health' as a way of not dealing with painful issues. This is seen sometimes when a client presents with one problem but other deeper concerns come to light. The client may feel a relief from the presenting problem and not wish to pursue the under-lying problems that the counsellor is aware may have caused, or exacerbated, the anxiety or depression, for instance. There may be a frustration for the counsellor if the client does not wish to explore the underlying causes or perpetuating factors of his problem, but it may not be the right time for the client to do this. If the client is happy with the process of counselling, he may return either to the same counsellor or to another counsellor when he feels able to deal with the underlying causes of his problem. It sometimes helps a counsellor to think of the client as being on a counselling journey and that we accompany our client for part of this journey but he may at any time decide to ask someone else to travel with him or even travel alone for some distance.

> **Example**   *A client had been sent by his doctor for counselling because he was suffering from frequent headaches. All the investigations had failed to uncover any physical cause of the headaches. It appeared upon questioning that these headaches started on a Friday evening and lasted over the weekend. Further probing revealed that the client visited his mother every Friday evening, and the client admitted some angry feelings towards his mother. At this point the client said that he felt perfectly well now that he knew the cause, and he wished to end counselling. The counsellor did not think that the client had allowed himself to express his feelings towards his mother but respected the client's wishes. This 'flight into health' by a client was frustrating for the counsellor, but the client was not ready to explore his feelings in any depth.*

Some clients may find it too difficult to explore endings in any depth and may deliberately speed through the ending of counselling in order to avoid painful feelings or challenges. This kind of client may bring up the topic of ending right at the finish of a session and, while expressing gratitude to the counsellor for the help received, be seen to almost run out of the door.

A more serious situation that needs to be recognized by the counsellor is when a depressed and possibly suicidal client suddenly states that he is feeling much better. This is always a warning sign because it may indicate that the client is feeling peaceful because he is actually going to commit suicide. Nearly always the client will give a clue to his real state of mind, because the will to live is immensely strong. If you are suspicious about a sudden improvement in a very depressed client, it is best to confront it and ask him when and how he decided to kill himself (Cummings and Sayana, 1995). If you are wrong you can apologize, but if you are right you may have saved a life.

Key practice point and questions

1 How would you recognize 'flight into health'?
2 How could you suggest to the client that he might benefit from further counselling without diminishing his achievements?
3 Be cautious if a seriously depressed client suddenly seems vastly improved with no apparent psychological reason.

Counsellor reluctance to terminate

There may be friction between counsellor and client if the counsellor finds it difficult to let go of a client who wishes to end counselling. The counsellor may see this as 'premature' and express her opinion that the client would do well to continue in order to work out concerns that have been uncovered or half-uncovered. It can be frustrating for a counsellor to know that there are further issues that may not be dealt with. The client may oblige in order to please the counsellor but this may conflict with his desire to end, and an uneasy situation may arise when the client wishes to pull away but does not wish to upset the counsellor. It is better to respect the client's judgement because it may not be the right time for the client to explore further.

Example A client explained that he had had some counselling in order to explore some marital difficulties. He was happy to look at some of his recent past and his part in the failure of his marriage. He felt he had learned a lot about himself and wanted to end the sessions. However, his counsellor suggested to him that in order to understand himself fully he should really explore his childhood and his relationship to his parents in greater depth. This the client did not wish to do at this time but did not want to upset his counsellor. With a tremendous effort he told her at the next session that he was sorry but he really did wish to end the counselling. This the counsellor reluctantly accepted but *urged the client to come back for some more sessions 'when he felt able to'. The client felt both exhilarated and annoyed. He felt good because he had been assertive, stated his wishes, and acted on them. He had also been the one to finish a relationship, whereas in the past it had always been the woman who had walked out on him. However, he also felt understandably annoyed that he had felt under pressure to continue. He also was unable to share with the counsellor the triumph he felt at standing up for himself.*

Sometimes the counsellor may have difficulty ending the counselling because the client is someone who is enjoyable to be with. It is a strange fact that as the client becomes happier and more pleasant company, so we as counsellors bid him farewell. It is hard to say goodbye to someone with whom we have worked intensely and shared much. As Kottler (1990: 109) states, 'saying goodbye to a client is so bittersweet that many therapists encounter difficulty letting go'. There can be much sadness for us mingled with the contentment of satisfaction for their achievement. It takes a special skill or psychological maturity to give so much to a client and then let them go with our best wishes.

***Example** A counsellor told me of an experience she had when she was a client. Apparently after about ten sessions and a gap of about four weeks during the Christmas break the counsellor suggested to the client that she had obviously coped very well during the break and perhaps, now the counselling had finished, a friendship could start instead. Although the client felt flattered that her counsellor had asked her for friendship she actually felt dismayed because she did not feel that she had coped at all well, had missed the sessions badly and was having nightmares. The client felt that she needed counselling rather than a friendship. Because the client felt that the situation was awkward and that the counsellor had misread all the signals, she left and found another counsellor. A friendship with the original counsellor did not develop. Upon reflection the client felt angry that the original counsellor had not handled the situation in a professional manner.*

Another difficulty may arise when the client expresses a wish to end but the counsellor insists on a 'termination process'. In some counselling orientations the ending of counselling is seen as immensely important and a certain number of sessions are allocated for dealing with the ending. There is no doubt that termination can bring up old and new issues for a client and some time needs to be allocated for this. However, a compliant client may agree to several sessions in order to please the counsellor but feel unhappy about this. One client told me that she had agreed to attend five sessions to look at the termination of the counselling after she had stated to the counsellor that she wished to stop attending. The client did not find these five sessions helpful and felt resentful towards the counsellor for insisting on them. Apparently the counsellor kept asking about the sadness that the client 'should' be feeling, when all the time the client was actually feeling angry that she had to pay for extra sessions that she did not want.

It is important to consider economic reasons for the counsellor to resist terminating the counselling. If the counsellor is working in a private practice, there is the grim reality of bills to be paid and a possible understandable tendency to hold on to the source of income. This is an area that each counsellor needs to explore for herself, while realizing that there are ethical considerations (explored further in Chapter 8). As 'word of mouth' is the best form of advertisement it is perhaps better long-term financial acumen to avoid clinging to unwilling clients but rather to celebrate their achievements and keep an open door for any future sessions.

Key practice questions

1   Do you find it difficult to let go of your clients?
2   Do you expect every client to undergo a termination process?
3   Are financial pressures overriding ethical considerations?

Goodbye letters

It may be helpful for some clients to write goodbye letters to the counsellor either in the ending sessions, or afterwards. It can be more strengthening to some clients to actually write down their gains from counselling and also their feelings about the loss of their counsellor.

Example *A client I saw over a period of eighteen months unexpectedly had the opportunity of a very good job in a* *different part of the country. She had made many changes in her life and had worked very hard at understanding herself and her needs. However the ending process had to be quicker than either of us wanted because of her imminent move. I indicated to her that I would be happy to hear how she was doing if she wanted to write to me. After about two months I received a letter telling me all her news and how, although she missed the sessions, she had learned about her own psychological resources and ways of coping. This was her way of terminating the counselling.*

One counsellor mentioned that she encouraged former clients to write to her and let her know how they were. She receives letters usually at six-monthly or yearly intervals for several years and gains much satisfaction from hearing about their progress. The clients feel that she was not just doing a job but genuinely cared to hear about them afterwards. Other therapists also encourage the client to write letters after the ending of therapy, sometimes up to five years (Maholick and Turner, 1979).

In cognitive-analytic therapy (Ryle, 1991) 'goodbye' letters are written by both client and therapist. There are usually twelve to sixteen sessions, and in the penultimate session the client is invited to bring a written evaluation of the sessions while the therapist brings a draft letter of her evaluation that the client will read and comment on. This enables the client to review his progress and discuss any unresolved feelings. The final exchange of letters is then a record of what has been achieved in therapy and a highlighting of what still requires to be attended to.

Key practice point

Goodbye letters can be written by client and counsellor as a way of recording what has been achieved in counselling, what has still to be looked at, and a way of saying goodbye.

Intermittent or sporadic counselling

Sometimes it is not possible to have neat weekly sessions with a structured ending, because of the nature of a client's work situation. Some clients may work shifts or have periods of work abroad, or in various parts of the country, for example airline staff or actors. With these clients it may be that there are periods of counselling sessions and then several weeks gap, and this may prove to be somewhat frustrating for both client and counsellor.

One of the problems with sporadic or intermittent counselling is that of continuity. If the client has had several sessions and then there is a gap of several weeks, it can take a while for both client and counsellor to re-orient themselves. There is always the added concern for the counsellor that if a particularly difficult problem is tackled, the client might then have to go for several weeks before he is able to attend the next counselling session. The ending of counselling may also be problematic and may take place in one session.

> **Example** *A client being seen by a counsellor is an actor and so goes all over the country in order to find work. His problem is one of bereavement in that he lost several of his family within a short time. He has to contain his grief while he is working. One of the priorities for him was to look at his coping mechanisms and resources to enable him to allow some of the feelings to be released in a manageable way. Fortunately, he was able to remember the release he felt when he allowed himself to paint and write a diary. This also helped to provide some continuity between sessions.*

Key practice questions

1 How can you provide continuity in sporadic counselling?
2 How can a satisfactory termination of counselling be achieved?

Final termination

Some counsellors believe that a final termination is essential for learning purposes. The reasoning behind this is the knowledge that endings are an intrinsic and inescapable part of life and that going through a termination of counselling leading to a final end may help the client when he has to face other endings in his life. Maholick and Turner (1979: 584) state that the termination of therapy is 'a preparation for being able to deal more adequately and openly with future goodbyes'. The existentialist counsellor would stress that all things do end – in death. This belief that a final ending is essential for clients to learn how to deal with other endings needs to be flexible to take into account those clients who may already have been traumatized by a series of final endings and perhaps need to learn that some endings need not be so abrupt.

Key practice question

Have you explored your thoughts and feelings about finality and death and how these may affect your attitudes in counselling?

Unhelpful reasons for not ending with a client

Sometimes it is useful to consider 'preposterous' concepts such as the following list in order to touch upon a possible truth.

1   I'm in private practice and I need the money.
2   I need the experience of working with long-term clients.
3   The client has issues that need to be worked on, although he disagrees.
4   I eagerly look forward to his sessions and I'm not ready to end.
5   All clients need many sessions looking at the issues of termination.
6   I know my client has problems with endings and I don't want to hurt him.
7   I have problems with endings.
8   I cannot face my own grief or my client's grief.

Summary

1   If the client ends the counselling process abruptly, the counsellor may be left with a sense of 'unfinished business'. An initial contract should be made between counsellor and client about procedures regarding missed appointments and follow-on appointments.

2   There may be feelings of frustration for the counsellor if he
    or she thinks that the client has ended prematurely. How-
    ever, if an open-door policy for future counselling sessions
    can be operated, the client may be able to work on more
    issues at a later time.

3   Breaks due to holidays or illness may precipitate an ending
    of the counselling or produce powerful feelings such as
    rejection for the client.

4   Termination may take one session or many sessions
    depending on the client's need.

5   Dependent clients may need a lot of reassurance about their
    progress in counselling and how the intensity of their
    demands may strain relationships.

6   Some clients may suffer intense bereavement feelings when
    counselling ends and may need to work on this further.

7   There may be a 'flight into health' by a client who does not
    wish to explore more deeply.

8   The counsellor may insist on a certain number of 'termi-
    nation' sessions that the client does not want.

9   'Goodbye' letters written by the client can be very useful as a
    way of ending counselling, recording progress and celebrat-
    ing achievements.

10 Some counsellors have a final ending. Some counsellors
    prefer an open-door policy so that the client may return in
    the future.

11 If you are unable to offer to see the client in the future for
    further work if it should be necessary, it is useful to explore
    other counselling options for the client.

7

Good Endings

This chapter looks at how we as counsellors can help to make the ending of counselling a good experience for both client and counsellor. Usually, some kind of review is important, whether it be formal as in a goal-attainment approach (Sutton, 1989) or informal where either the client or counsellor sums up the work that has been achieved in counselling. The goal-attainment approach is where goals are negotiated and agreed with the client and the client is invited to evaluate his progress using a scale from -5 to $+5$. There are creative interventions, such as the use of drawing, poetry, modelling, that can also be used to evaluate the counselling in a more innovative way.

Satisfactory endings

A satisfactory ending happens when both client and counsellor feel content with the counselling experience, having acknowledged the work accomplished by both of them and the gains that have been made by the client, which results in a sense of completion. Often the client will make the suggestion that he has achieved what he wanted and that he thinks that he does not need any more counselling. It is helpful to instigate a review of the counselling, how the client was at the beginning, what gains have been made, how he is now, and what may still need to be worked on in the future. Counselling does not solve all problems for everybody for evermore, but the client can take with him a greater understanding of his own inner resources that can help him cope better with future difficulties. The client will, one hopes, be looking forward to his life ahead rather than fearfully looking backwards.

Example   *A client came when she was experiencing high stress levels that had been accumulating over many years. She had a handicapped daughter, a full-time job and was coping well until everything seemed to be an enormous effort and she was becoming tired and irritable. Over about a dozen sessions she was able to explore her feelings about her daughter and also her belief that she must cope totally on her own and not accept help from anyone. As she began to feel better and more able to enjoy her life she began to talk about ending counselling. She reviewed her own progression through counselling, and it seemed that she felt good about ending but she wanted one more follow-up session in order to 'touch base'.*

Discussion   *This ending felt extremely satisfying for both client and counsellor. The client initiated the ending process, asked for a review session and then for a follow-up session. She had achieved everything that she wanted from counselling.*

In the following example the counsellor involved said that the experience felt satisfying because 'it all felt worthwhile' and she felt that she had made a difference in this client's life.

Example   *The client presented with a history of depression. On exploring her childhood it was discovered that nobody appeared to have taken much notice of her, she felt worthless, and she blamed herself for everything. Over a period of two years, being seen weekly, she was able to become more self-confident, pursued some interests outside the home, divorced her husband and found a satisfying job. The counsellor saw this client blossom from a self-absorbed, 'boring' person into someone who began to be able to express herself and not only care for herself but also for other people.*

Discussion   *This client was shown respect by her counsellor and learned to respect herself. The client was able to learn how to change the way she perceived the world. The counsellor felt that the whole process had been a shared creative endeavour.*

There have been several conceptualizations of satisfactory endings. Kupers (1988) believes that no-one has surpassed Freud's analysis of the criteria for termination. Freud states that there are three requirements for a satisfactory ending: firstly, that the symptoms have disappeared, secondly, that these symptoms will not reappear and thirdly, that there would not be any further significant change if the client were to continue (Freud, 1937). It may not be possible to meet all of these criteria in brief counselling, but Freud's conceptualizations of termination give us clear guidelines for achieving satisfaction both for the client and counsellor.

In an imperfect world Freud's criteria for termination have been modified. Maholick and Turner (1979) opted for observation of reduction of initial symptoms, increased understanding and valuing of self and others, with increased ability to cope and enjoy life. Many counsellors and clients feel satisfied if the clients learn more productive methods for dealing with or managing symptoms and enhancing their enjoyment of life.

Creative endings

Endings can be fun and/or joyful. Some clients will respond to a suggestion to make the ending session more playful. This can be achieved through using art materials such as paints or coloured pens, plasticine, a collection of stones, buttons or coins, or by encouraging the client to write a poem. The collection of objects, such as stones, can be useful because the stones can be of differing sizes, shapes, colours and textures and the client can choose which stones he wishes to represent his progression through counselling. Both client and counsellor can let their imaginations run free in order to find the best creative ending for their work together.

If the client is open to the idea of using paints or coloured pens, he could draw a series of pictures of what counselling has meant to him. It is a graphic way of reviewing the counselling and it can extend into a possible future scenario. I have found it useful to say to my clients in all honesty that I am not an artist and have never learnt to draw. Then the client feels free to play with the colours and draw stick-people without fear. Some clients of course would not like this idea.

Example   *A client drew a series of pictures to show how he had opened out emotionally during counselling and had been able to explore parts of himself that he had previously locked away. His first picture showed a small figure that was huddled and frightened while others around him were happy and laughing. The last picture showed a man with his arms outstretched, sharing his happiness with all his family and friends.*

Some clients may respond better to objects that they can touch and move. This is where some plasticine or a collection of stones or other objects may be used. Again, the client may wish to portray his progress through counselling. A collection of objects, from which the client is free to choose, can be used to show how he sees a change, for instance in relationships with others, or a change in himself. The only problem in using plasticine or objects is that the client cannot take them home, whereas a picture could be taken away.

Example   *A client chose various kinds of stones from the counsellor's collection to demonstrate how he had changed his relationship with his wife. First, he put the stones in a representation of how it had been for him when he first came for counselling. This showed him with a space between him and his family, and he described how he had felt outside the family and not involved. As he learnt some communication skills and how to express how he felt, so he began to feel part of the family, and his second positioning of the stones reflected his rejoining the family and standing beside his wife.*

Some clients are able to express themselves in written words and have possibly kept a journal of their progress. One way of ending counselling may be for the client to re-read his first entries and either show the counsellor or talk about how he felt at the beginning of counselling and how things have changed for him. A few clients find that they can express their feelings in poetry, maybe for the first time, and they may like to write a poem or some prose about the ending of their counselling journey.

Example   *Here is an extract from one such poem:*

I came a wreck – trembling with fear and trepidation.
You sat there so calm.
You listened.
And I could pour out my story in safety.
And I too started to listen instead of screaming.
And I found a way through where there had not been a path.
You encouraged me and supported me
Until I could stand proudly and stride forwards into my future.

The following extract is from a poem which was written by a client who very much wanted a good ending to her counselling because many endings for her had been painful. When she wrote this poem she knew that the counselling had to finish because she was moving house, and she wanted to honour what had happened for her and share her appreciation in this creative way.

> *Pas de Deux*
> How the movement
>   of our dance has changed.
> Before, I was the one
>   who struggled to keep in time
>   and get the routine right.
> Sometimes I danced around you,
>   never approaching,
>   never touching . . .
>
> I scarcely saw *you* dance at all,
>   and yet I was aware you moved
>   gently and steadily
>   sometimes a little closer, but
>   always within this containing space of ours
>
> You have come alive for me
>   and now I can observe
>   your solo too
>   and marvel at the intricacies of how you move.
> The beat has quickened
>   and an increased
>   urgency has speeded up our steps.
>
> How will the final curtain fall?
>   I ask myself . . .

Perhaps a little out of breath
and yet with feelings of accomplishment
the ending chords will
bid us turn and for the last time
honour our partner
before we say 'Good-bye'.

L.J.

If you as a counsellor tape your client sessions, that may be another way of successfully reviewing the counselling. If the client would like to, both counsellor and client could listen to an early tape and then one of the later tapes in order to hear the improvement in life circumstances. Sometimes it is possible to hear a difference in the client's voice, self-confidence and clarity of thinking. Some counsellors tape sessions and encourage clients to work on the tapes during sessions, so that this idea would seem natural to them. Albert Ellis advises the client to record sessions in order to work on them between sessions and after counselling has ended (Dryden, 1990: 99). A few counsellors may use video-taping where again the client would have the opportunity to view one of the beginning tapes and then one of the ending tapes in order to review progress. Video-tapes have the advantage over audio-tapes in that it is possible to observe body language and posture, which may indicate more clearly the progress that the client has made.

Celebrating endings

Celebrating an ending can be seen as recognizing achievement. For so many people it is difficult to acknowledge our successes and receive compliments. As counsellors, not only do we have to learn the art of receiving gratitude from clients gracefully but also we need to encourage our clients to acknowledge their own hard work and achievements.

If an ending is made into a special occasion then it can act like a springboard for new ventures. Instead of seeing counselling as 'something that was necessary but I should really have coped on my own', if the client can acknowledge the gains he has made and the understanding that has been achieved, both of himself and other people, then he can begin to feel more confidence in himself and his life process. A client may see that what he thought was the worst part of his life has actually compelled him to learn more about himself, and so he may become clearer in his thinking and more mature in his behaviour.

Although some clients will believe that their counselling sessions have helped them at a particularly difficult part of their lives, and that they have gained in the process, there are also some clients who will find that their whole direction in life has changed as a result of entering counselling. There are some clients who have been helped to discover parts of themselves that were hidden, for instance, the client who discovered a deep compassion for other people that had been hidden below his own unexpressed grief, and found that he had a gift for healing. M. Scott Peck describes this process of 'clearing the decks' in a poetic way – 'God creates each soul differently, so that when all the mud is finally cleared away, His light will shine through it in a beautiful, colourful, totally new pattern' (Peck, 1990: 303). And so some clients have enriched their own lives and the lives of those around them. As a counsellor I feel immensely privileged to be allowed to be part of this process. It is good to celebrate the growth of an individual.

There are some clients who are so enthralled with the whole process and result of counselling that they resolve to become counsellors themselves. If a client feels enthused with the idea of counselling and finds a talent for it, then that is an excellent reason for taking up counselling as a career. Of course the cynics in the profession could speculate here about the possibility of dependency issues.

Some clients may wish to celebrate the ending of counselling with a present for the counsellor as a way of showing their gratitude. It is generally seen to be acceptable for the counsellor to receive small gifts, although some counsellors may choose never to do so. Windy Dryden describes how he accepts 'a gift with gratitude as long as its value in monetary terms is not highly disproportionate to the occasion' (Dryden, 1990: 88). I myself have received a few gifts such as a bunch of flowers, some candles, a delicious cake, a box of chocolates. It would seem churlish to refuse such spontaneous gestures of gratitude. However, I did turn down an invitation to a champagne supper. There could be difficulties if the client were to offer money or expensive gifts. The BAC Code of Ethics and Practice for Counsellors states that counsellors must not exploit clients financially (BAC, 1996a: B.2.2.6).

What constitutes a good ending?

We may say (with acknowledgement to the students of the Thameslink/UEL Counselling Diploma Course) that a good ending has the following attributes:

1 structured ending
2 choice
3 a chance to express feelings
4 celebration.

A good ending is one that is planned and structured so that neither counsellor nor client is taken unawares by an unprepared sudden termination of counselling. The client needs to have a choice in what is to happen as regards the ending of counselling, whether that be for him to end counselling because the work is finished or to continue elsewhere because the counselling contract has ended. There needs to be space for the client to explore the feelings that arise as the counselling ends. There also needs to be time to celebrate the progress that the client has made during the counselling.

ABC of termination considerations in counselling
- A = acknowledgement of *achievement*.
- B = *balance* between what has been achieved and what has yet to be worked on.
- C = *choices* for client and counsellor.

A is for acknowledgement of achievement – looking at where the client was at the start of counselling and what the problem areas were and where the client is in the present and what developments have been made.

B is for balancing what has been achieved with an acknowledgement of what has yet to be worked on, either in the present counselling relationship or in future relationships. It may be that the imminent ending of counselling has precipitated deep feelings about ending which need to be acknowledged and worked through. Acknowledgement of work to be tackled in the future is extremely important when referral is being discussed.

C is for choices when client and counsellor discuss the possibilities and alternatives that are available to the client. Choice is important in endings because of the deep pain that can be felt if the decision to end is one-sided. A client may feel rejection or abandonment if the counsellor unilaterally decides to refer the client on. A counsellor may feel bewildered and self-blaming if the client unilaterally decides to end counselling. However, as professional counsellors we have to honour this particular client choice and deal with our own feelings in supervision. Choice is important in referral so that both client and counsellor feel satisfied that the best plan of action has been executed.

Summary

1 Endings can be a time for acknowledgement and celebration of achievement.
2 Creativity in the form of drawing, writing, poetry and play can help to make an ending a positive experience.

8

Ethical Considerations regarding Referral and Termination Issues

This chapter explores in greater depth some of the ethical concerns that may arise in counselling and supervision. There are the possible dilemmas arising from a client who is at risk of harming himself or others. There are considerations about referring to friends and how to monitor our own competence levels, financial needs and emotional needs. Dual relationships and relationships with former clients are explored. What happens if the client complains about referral or termination? And finally the use of supervision for counsellors is upheld.

What to do if the client is, or is contemplating, harming self or others

It is vital to assess the risk of actual harm to self or others. If the client mentions the possibility of suicide it is always important to find out how serious the intention is. Some clients have suicidal thoughts which may even be comforting as a possible escape route, others may have suicidal thoughts but know that they would never actually kill themselves, and others may have planned every detail and be very serious about their intentions. If the client cannot promise not to kill himself then action will have to be taken, either with the client's permission or without. Although ultimately it is the client's choice to end his life or not, we can hope that the wish to die is a temporary situation and help the client through this time as best we can. Sometimes problems can appear so overwhelming that suicide seems the only solution, but upon exploration the client can begin to separate out problems and find alternative outcomes (Bond, 1993).

Example   *A counsellor saw a client for a few sessions and he appeared to be slightly depressed and anxious since his wife had left him. However, he seemed to have good coping abilities and was seeing his doctor regularly for extra support. At one session he came in and talked normally, but it soon became apparent that all was not well. He had received divorce papers through the post that morning and was in a state of shock. As he talked he revealed that he could not seem to feel anything except extreme fear. He then revealed that he was profoundly depressed and he told the counsellor that he was misusing the drugs he had been given and could not promise not to ingest all of them. Upon probing he said that he could see no reason for living and he could not promise that he would not kill himself. He had no friends or family. As the counsellor was working in a GP surgery it was an easy matter to consult the doctor on call, and the client was examined and taken into a psychiatric unit immediately. This was the best solution for him. He was persuaded to take an anti-depressant, he was looked after, there were people to talk to, and he quickly gained his equilibrium. The counsellor saw him afterwards, and he was feeling much better and was looking towards a new future for himself.*

If you are working privately, it is prudent to take details of the clients' doctors in case of emergency. However, some clients may not wish to either give their GP's name nor for him or her to be contacted by you. Some counsellors also liaise with a psychiatrist. This is useful if you feel that a psychiatric assessment is indicated, and the client has agreed. If there is no private arrangement with a psychiatrist, the client can only be referred back to his GP. If you are working in a GP surgery you can either contact the client's GP directly or there will be an emergency doctor available.

The Code of Ethics and Practice for Counsellors (BAC, 1996a) states that 'Exceptional circumstances may arise which give the counsellor good grounds for believing that the client will cause serious physical harm to others or themselves, or have harm caused to him/her. In such circumstances the client's consent to a change in the agreement about confidentiality should be sought whenever posssible unless there are also good grounds for believing the client is no longer able to take responsibility for his/her own actions' (BAC, 1996a: B.4.4.). Taking on board the responsibility we have as counsellors in the event of threatened self-harm or harming others, we need to plan carefully how we can best cope with these eventualities. We may need to break confidentiality in order to prevent a suicide or a crime involving harm to others. If we do nothing, then we are in danger of committing the offence of being an accomplice to suicide (Bond, 1993). In the USA counsellors may be prosecuted if they fail to warn or take action when someone is in danger (Jenkins, 1997). Some counsellors will discuss under what circumstances confidentiality may be broken, with all clients in the first session. However, it is then possible that clients may not feel free to talk about any violent thoughts they may be having, and often permission to explore and express the suicidal or aggressive thoughts and feelings is sufficient for the client to learn how to understand and deal with them. Other counsellors only discuss a possible break of confidentiality if the need arises.

Dealing with a client who has thoughts of suicide or harming others is obviously difficult for the counsellor. There may be the need for immediate action or a more long-term 'holding' and supporting, with extra sessions if needed. Sometimes a contract made with the client promising not to harm himself may need to be renewed from session to session, or the counsellor can stipulate that the client must undertake not to commit suicide whilst receiving counselling. Supervisory support is certainly necessary, and confidential discussion with colleagues for their experience and support may be useful. There may be a desire on the counsellor's part to offer the client too much in terms of support, such as the counsellor's home phone number, to the detriment of the counsellor herself. It can be more helpful to help the client find more resources, such as any self-help groups, the Samaritans, friends and family.

Key practice point

While respecting the client's right to choose to commit suicide, we must do all within our power to help the client or persuade the client to accept the appropriate help for him (Szasz, 1986).

Referring to friends and colleagues

It is human nature to recommend the services of those we know. There would be a problem if, as counsellors, we only referred clients to friends and disregarded everyone else because we did not know them. However, it seems that we may be influenced in our choice of referral sources because of an identification with particular elements such as ethnic or religious background, similar training and therapeutic experiences or personal history (Wood and Wood, 1990). Also it may be that someone has sent clients to us and we wish to reciprocate, or we may refer to another professional hoping that he or she will return the favour at some future date.

It is our professional duty to be aware of the expertise that is available in our area. If we feel that it is in the best interests of our clients that we know more about the professional to whom we wish to refer, that could be a very good reason to instigate some 'getting to know you' meetings which could lead to greater knowledge of what is available in the local vicinity and a closer liaison between professionals. The BAC Code of Ethics and Practice for Counsellors is concerned that counsellors do not exploit their clients, so if a counsellor considers the client's interests and sincerely believes that a friend will provide the services that the client needs, then there is no ethical problem. 'Counsellors must not exploit clients financially, sexually, emotionally or in any other way' (BAC, 1996a: B.2.2.6). Of course there could be a potential problem for the friendship if the client does not approve of our referral choice, so if at all possible it is good to be able to recommend several people so that the client may choose.

Key practice question

If we refer clients to friends and/or colleagues are we doing the best for our clients?

Dual relationships

There are possible ethical problems involved when a counsellor is asked to give counselling to someone that they have known before in another context. For instance, there may be a working relationship, social relationship or training relationship. It is the responsibility of the counsellor to set the boundaries between counselling and any other relationship and to refer to another counsellor if this seems to be the most appropriate action. The BAC Code of Ethics and Practice for Trainers states that 'former trainees must not become clients, nor former clients become trainees, until a period of time has elapsed for reflection and after consultation with a counselling supervisor' (BAC, 1997: B.1.7). Likewise, supervisors themselves must clearly draw the line between supervision and personal counselling for their supervisees. The Code of Ethics and Practice for Supervisors of Counsellors states that 'a supervisor must not have a counselling supervision and a personal counselling contract with the same supervisee over the same period of time' (BAC, 1996b: B.1.6). The ethical dilemmas presented by dual relationships are particularly likely in smaller towns and rural areas where social, working and training interactions are more probable than in large cities.

When the counselling has finished, the counsellor is accountable for any change in the relationship, whether it be in business, social or training contexts. This must be discussed in supervision, with particular emphasis on any power dynamics being resolved. There can be particular difficulties if the client wishes to see the counsellor again in the future for more sessions and this may not be possible if the relationship between counsellor and client has altered.

Occasionally, as counsellors, we may be asked to give counselling to members of the same family. This may cause problems with confidentiality, if for instance we were to counsel a husband and wife separately, or a mother and daughter. The problems that a client presents may involve the other person, so in general it is better to refer the other family member. Sometimes it is useful to let a partner, for instance, sit in on a session so that you can observe the dynamics operating between the client and his or her partner but this would be for your client's benefit. If family therapy or couple therapy is indicated then a referral to another counsellor would be suitable.

Key practice points

1 It is the responsibility of the counsellor to set the boundaries between counselling and any other relationship.
2 It is usually better to refer a partner or another member of a client's family to a different counsellor.

Financial issues for the counsellor

Some counsellors work in a voluntary capacity, while other counsellors are working full-time and trying to earn a living. There may be a temptation (which may or may not be conscious) for private counsellors to encourage clients to continue in counselling because of financial reasons. As Rowe (1991) succinctly says, 'Where a therapist makes his living from doing therapy, it is not in his financial interests to finish therapy.' This could lead to a counsellor's not tackling a dependency problem with the client, or encouraging the client to increase the frequency of sessions or stay in counselling longer than is necessary. The client's needs, which may include looking at termination issues, are not being met. Worse still the counsellor may encourage a client's addiction to counselling, as 'keeping a client locked into treatment, with no hope or wish for escape, can ensure a therapist a lifetime income' (Kottler, 1990). This undesirable state of affairs does not allow the client to become independent of the counsellor.

Other dubious financial areas concern the receiving of payment for passing on referrals. Stout (1993) writes of cases in the USA where therapists have received payments from hospitals and other professionals for referring clients. It is difficult to believe that the client's best interests are being met in these cases.

The clearest method of dealing with the financial aspects of counselling is to draw up a contract with the client. In this way, if the counsellor charges for missed sessions or holiday time, the client is made fully aware of this at the beginning and does not receive a nasty shock. Likewise, if there is likely to be an increase in fees, the client should be told of this too at the beginning of counselling. The counsellor needs to have a clear policy in situations where the client can no longer afford the fees. Some counsellors operate a sliding scale of fees and some will accept other services. Some counsellors would refer the client to other counselling services which may be free or less expensive. It is not normally good policy to allow the client to incur debts. There can be much unnecessary anxiety as well as ethical concern that occurs for both counsellor and client when the financial arrangements are not clear (Sills, 1997).

Key practice points

1 Financial considerations may prevent the counsellor from attending to the client's dependency problems and termination difficulties.
2 Financial commitments for the client must be made clear at the beginning of the counselling contract.

Emotional issues for the counsellor

As counsellors, there is a necessity to monitor our own emotional needs and to make sure that these are being met outside the counselling arena. However, it is evident that being a counsellor does produce the satisfaction of working with and helping people to the best of our ability, and most of our clients are very grateful for our efforts. It is always useful to periodically check with ourselves what we are expecting from our counselling work and our clients, what aspects of the work we find satisfactory and what parts we struggle with. Bond (1993) suggests that the counsellor's need is not a problem 'if the need is complementary to the client's use of counselling'. So if the counsellor is aware, for example, of her vulnerability, then this can be used productively within the counselling relationship in order to help the client understand himself and his relationship with others in a fuller way. A problem will arise if the counsellor is unaware of her own emotional needs and the client is being used to supply these. For example, a counsellor may feel unable to help a client make an appropriate referral or to end counselling because she does not wish to end the counselling relationship.

If a client arouses strong feelings in a counsellor then the counsellor needs to discover whether this is an old pattern of the client's being re-enacted or whether the feelings are originating in the counsellor, or both. Counselling supervision may help to clarify the situation, and if necessary the counsellor may need to receive some therapy herself. Most counsellors do not wish to use the feelings generated within the therapeutic relationship as the basis for a friendship, for as one respondent to the questionnaire (Appendix 1) stated, 'It does not work.' A counselling relationship is formed in order to benefit the client, and however difficult it may be for a counsellor to let go of a client, this is the natural end to a counselling encounter. Counselling should enable the client to improve his life outside the counselling arena rather than its taking over his life. The BAC Code of Ethics and Practice for Counsellors states that 'counsellors must not exploit clients financially, sexually, emotionally or in any other way' (BAC, 1996a: B.2.2.6).

Key practice questions

1   What satisfactions do you gain from counselling?
2   Are you holding on to clients longer than is necessary because of your own emotional needs?
3   Do you have satisfying relationships separate from your working life that supply your need to be needed, emotional intimacy and sharing, the giving and receiving of affection?

Relationships with former clients

There are some counsellors who may continue a relationship with their clients after the counselling has finished. Although most counsellors do not become friends with previous clients (see Appendix 1, Question 18), occasionally it happens. There are some mixed views amongst counsellors on the wisdom of a friendship between counsellors and former clients. Generally, most counsellors realize that no matter how equal in humanity a counsellor and client may be, there is still an inequality in a relationship where one person is seeking guidance or treatment from another and also often paying for this service. The counselling relationship is for the benefit of the client and examining the needs of the client and is not like the sharing that is usual in a friendship. Moreover, as Lakin (1988: 68) states, 'the tensions of disappointed or unmet needs remain obstacles to egalitarian relationships even after therapy is terminated'.

Some counsellors who believe that the relationship between counsellor and client is the most important factor in the counselling process may be more likely to continue the relationship beyond the end of counselling. Counsellors working in the person-centred way talk of reaching a stage of real mutuality with their clients. Mutuality is where the counsellor and the client become 'transparent' to one another during the counselling, and the client knows the counsellor as well as the counsellor knows the client. Mearns and Thorne (1988: 146) ask the question, 'Why then are they not free to continue a relationship as friends once the counselling process is ended?' The BAC Code of Ethics and Practice for Counsellors advises caution for any change in the relationship.

There are strict ethical codes against sexual relationships with clients. This is because clients may experience deep emotional distress and turmoil at the time and afterwards, and then subsequently have difficulties with trust, boundaries, suppressed rage, guilt and suicidal feelings (Bond, 1993; Russell, 1993; Rutter, 1991). Some prohibitions regarding relationships with ex-clients have been considered, such as a period of at least twelve weeks to have passed between the ending of the counselling and any sexual relationship. If the counselling has been in depth, involves transference, or has been long-lasting, it is thought to be harmful to the client if sexual relationships take place at any time between counsellor and client even after a gap of several years.

Key practice points

1 Most counsellors do not make friends with former clients, because of the inherent inequality of the relationship.
2 Sexual relationships with a client can be severely damaging for the client and are against all ethical codes of conduct for a professional.
3 Sexual relationships with an ex-client can be problematic because of the power inequality of the counselling relationship.

Competence and limitations

Sometimes there can be a thin line drawn between proven abilities in a certain area and the desire to gain experience. Some counsellors may be content to gain special training in a particular area, for instance alcohol counselling, and stay within that area. Other counsellors may wish to offer counselling to a variety of clients with differing problems and concerns and so gain a wider experience. However, there may come a time when a client presents with a difficulty that is intriguing although the counsellor may have little knowledge about it. There is also the possibility that the counsellor may have established a strong therapeutic relationship with the client and then the client presents with an underlying problem with which the counsellor has scant experience. The counsellor and her supervisor then have to decide whether or not to refer this client to someone with experience of the particular difficulty or whether the counsellor can deal with, and so gain experience of, this difficulty and this field of counselling. Sometimes the answer may be to refer the client to a practitioner experienced in that problem but to resolve to undergo further training or attend a course so that there would not necessarily be the need to refer in future instances. A situation like this may prove to be the impetus to seek further professional development; this is actively encouraged in the Code of Ethics and Practice for Counsellors, which states that 'counsellors should have received adequate basic training before commencing counselling, and should maintain ongoing professional development' (BAC, 1996a: B.2.4.2).

It is the duty of counsellors to be fully aware of their competence and limitations. The BAC Code of Ethics and Practice for Counsellors states that 'counsellors should monitor actively the limitations of their own competence through counselling supervision/consultative support, and by seeking the views of their clients and other counsellors. Counsellors should work within their own known limits' (BAC, 1996a: B.2.2.17). On the subject of referrals the BAC Code of Ethics and Practice for Counsellors states that 'it is an indication of the competence of counsellors when they recognize their inability to counsel a client or clients and make appropriate referrals' (BAC, 1996a: B.2.2.19). The competencies which can reasonably be expected of counsellors

---

Box 8.1   Referral competencies

The counsellor:

1 routinely assesses suitability of inward referral;
2 routinely notes the influence/assessment of inward referrer on client;
3 routinely and purposefully considers the possibility of the client's being better served elsewhere;
4 maintains a useful, accurate and broad database of referral information/resources;
5 makes meaningful contact with and gains (where possible) independent views on skills and specialisms of other practitioners and agencies;
6 makes ethical commitment to clients' welfare above her own financial and clinical interests;
7 updates her own knowledge of diagnostic criteria and research indications for treatments of choice;
8 honestly and accurately informs clients of her own competencies and limits;
9 develops and monitors the interpersonal skills required for sensitive referral suggestions;
10 becomes involved or remains neutral in the referral process as appropriate;
11 maintains ongoing contact and dual responsibility when appropriate;
12 evaluates the appropriateness and success of referral if practicable and ethically acceptable.

---

with regard to referral are listed in Box 8.1. I would like to add that I would hope that counsellors would always make appropriate referrals with care and sensitivity.

Client complaints about referral and termination

If a client has been referred to you and you find that the client is very unhappy about the circumstances of this referral, you will clearly need to thoroughly discuss the situation with the referred client. It may be that the counsellor concerned has not handled the referral appropriately in that the client was not consulted adequately, or that there are more serious possibilities of financial, emotional or sexual abuse by the counsellor. If the matter cannot be resolved, then it is sensible to discuss the situation with your supervisor. It may be necessary to talk with the counsellor concerned. If this step is not enough to resolve the problem, then the Complaints Procedure may have to be used either by you or the client. The BAC Code of Ethics and Practice for Counsellors states that 'if a counsellor suspects misconduct by another counsellor which cannot be resolved or remedied after discussion with the counsellor concerned, they should implement the Complaints Procedure, doing so without breaches of confidentiality other than those necessary for investigating the complaint' (BAC, 1996a: B.2.5.2). The client can also initiate a court action if he or she wishes legal sanctions or compensation.

> **Example** *A client went to see a male counsellor and told him that she had been given his name by her previous counsellor but was very unhappy about the way the referral had been arranged. It transpired that the client had seen a female counsellor for about ten sessions, and through the use of various Gestalt exercises had uncovered a history of maternal child abuse. The counsellor then explained that she only saw people on a short-term basis, and that the client would need to see someone else. The client felt extremely unhappy about this as she felt vulnerable and traumatized again. The counsellor gave the client a list of names and said that she was not available to see this client again.*
>
> *The new counsellor felt very concerned and angry at the way this client had been treated. He allowed her to fully express her distress and anger at what had happened and asked her what she wanted to do about the way she had been treated. The client thought about instigating a complaints procedure against her previous counsellor but did not feel strong enough to do so. With the client's agreement, and after consultation with his supervisor, the new counsellor wrote a letter to the previous counsellor expressing his concern at the way his client had been treated. The counsellor wrote back and apologized, explaining that she had not been well herself at the time but realized that the referral had been badly handled. The client felt satisfied by this apology and was then able to continue her counselling.*

Key practice points

1 If a client is unhappy about a previous counsellor's handling of a referral or termination, it is necessary to allow the client time to express his anger and distress.
2 Consult your supervisor after determining what the client wishes to happen.
3 Contact the counsellor concerned, or help your client to do so, if that is what your client wishes. Question – if your client does not wish to contact the counsellor, how do you address the issue of possible abuse by the counsellor or negligence?
4 If the situation cannot be resolved, instigate, or help your client to instigate, the BAC Complaints Procedure.

The use of supervision

Supervision for counsellors is essential. It is a BAC requirement that all practising counsellors have at least one and a half hours supervision (on a one-to-one basis or the equivalent in a group) per month, and more supervision if the case load is heavy. The purpose of counselling supervision is to provide a place where the counsellor can discuss her counselling and her clients.

It is useful to see supervision in terms of a formative, normative and restorative framework (Inskipp and Proctor, 1993). The restorative function of supervision is one of support and encouragement. The formative function of supervision is one of teaching and exploring the counselling that is being done. The normative function is the one concerning the ethical considerations of counselling and is where the responsibility of supervision of counselling is important.

If a counsellor is having difficulties with a referral issue or termination it is helpful to be reminded of the ethical requirements by a supervisor. The supervisor will also have a more objective view of the counsellor's limitations and can recommend a referral if necessary, and support the counsellor if there are any feelings of inadequacy. Another important role of the supervisor is the support offered when the supervisor recognizes that the beginning counsellor could continue with the client and does not 'insist that students refer cases within their skill level' (Erdman, 1994). On the questionnaire (Appendix 1) a high proportion of counsellors answered in the affirmative when asked if, with hindsight, they had continued with a client who would have been better referred to someone else. It is interesting to speculate whether or not the counsellor had discussed this particular client and the circumstances with their supervisor. The BAC Code of Ethics and Practice for Counsellors states that 'counsellors will, from time to time, find themselves caught between conflicting ethical principles. In these circumstances, they are urged to consider the particular situation in which they find themselves and to discuss the situation with their counselling supervisor and/or other experienced counsellors' (BAC, 1996a: B.8.1).

Key practice point

The use of supervision is essential for counsellors, especially if there is a concern about the possible need of a referral for a particular client.

Summary

1 After thoroughly exploring the actual risk of a client's harming himself or others, confidentiality may have to be broken in order to protect lives.

2 We must not use our clients to meet our own financial and emotional needs, to the detriment of the clients.

3 The idea of continuing relationships with former clients should be monitored – the question to ask ourselves is 'Why do I wish to be friends with this person?'

4 As professionals we have a duty to be aware of our limitations and to continuously update our knowledge.

5 We need to be aware of the procedure for client complaints.

6 Supervision is essential in order to provide a safe place for us to discuss our clients and any concerns that we have about our counselling.

9

Resources

This chapter looks at some of the personal resources of the counsellor which are vital if we are to avoid burnout. Also there are some suggestions for building a professional-resources directory.

Resources for the counsellor

A counsellor needs to monitor her own resources if she is to avoid premature termination of her counselling career. As counsellors, we do not have infinite resources, although the expectation that we do, or should have, is prevalent amongst carers. If we allow ourselves to become too depleted we run the risk of impaired judgement, and are more likely to have problems with knowing when to refer clients on. One of the easiest ways of determining whether or not we are caring for ourselves sufficiently is to ask ourselves the question, 'Do I have enough energy left to enjoy myself?'

Most counsellors know the 'correct' things to do in order to replenish their enthusiasm, but what makes us go beyond our limits and become ill? Sometimes there is a genuine difficulty in determining our warning signs and also then acting on them. Box 9.1 lists some questions to ask ourselves in order to monitor our limitations. Box 9.2 suggests some sources of encouragement for counsellors, while Box 9.3 lists some recommended books.

Know local, regional and national resources and keep up to date

Just over half of the counsellors who responded to Question 9 in the questionnaire (Appendix 1) indicated that they maintained an

---

Box 9.1   Questions to ask ourselves in order to monitor our limitations

1   Where do I feel tension in my body?
2   What happens physically if I ignore my tension (for instance, fatigue, headaches, gastrointestinal disturbances, pain, illness)?
3   If I am emotionally exhausted how does this affect me (for instance, irritation, tearfulness, apprehension, etc.)?
4   If I am mentally jaded how does this affect me (for instance, boredom, lethargy, lack of concentration, etc.)?
5   If I am spiritually disconnected do I recognize the symptoms (for instance, lack of joy and discovery, and loss of a sense of purpose and belonging)?
6   If I recognize my limitations, do I then push myself beyond them, and if so, why?
7   Can I forgive myself for my limitations?
8   Can I be kind to myself?

Box 9.2   Encouragement for counsellors

- Have I drawn up a list of fun activities?
- Have I allowed myself to have some fun?
- Have I explored humour and laughter?
- Have I recently planned to start something, not associated with counselling, I have always wanted to do?
- Have I thoroughly investigated stress management for myself (massage, aromatherapy, healing, yoga, meditation, tai chi, dancing, etc.)?
- Have I listed my good qualities?
- Have I acknowledged my successes?
- Have I rewarded myself recently?
- Have I considered some different areas of training?
- Do I want to supervise or teach?

---

up-to-date file of professionals' details in case they needed to make a referral. It is important to regularly review your resource file because the information regarding local facilities and even national organizations is constantly changing. There are some excellent information books available, often at the local library, such as *The Mental Health Handbook* (Drew and King, 1995) and *Help!* (Evans, 1996). Also telephone directories, *Yellow Pages* and *Thomson Local* have the details of national and local helplines.

Box 9.3   Recommended books

Burnard, P. (1991) *Coping with Stress in the Health Professions: A Practical Guide.* London: Chapman & Hall.

Fontana, D. (1989) *Managing Stress.* Leicester: BPS/Routledge.

Lewis, D. (1993) *One-Minute Stress Management.* London: Cedar.

LeShan, L. (1983) *How to Meditate.* Northamptonshire: Turnstone Press.

Palmer, S. and Dryden, W. (1995) *Counselling for Stress Problems.* London: Sage.

Some areas have formed a local organization for counsellors where information can be exchanged and study days can be arranged. This is an excellent way of keeping in touch with other counsellors and learning about their special interests and abilities in various areas of counselling. Also some areas offer an up-to-date directory of counsellors, psychotherapists and complementary therapists (for instance in Kent there is a free directory called *Kent Connexions* available three times a year).

It is important before referring to find out as much as possible about the individual, agency, organization or group. If an individual has received a good training he or she will be happy to give details of training, experience, specialist areas and membership of professional bodies. Most organizations have written information available. Most counsellors have prepared a written information sheet about themselves. Sometimes groups may offer very little counselling or may not have suitably qualified people acting as counsellors. There may be no cost involved for the client or there may be substantial cost. The client may be seen immediately or there may be long waiting lists.

Resource list and suggestions regarding the kinds of agencies to which to refer

These contact addresses represent a selection only but do present a good flavour of what is on offer and may be a starting point for your own referral lists. Some organizations may be able to offer regional contacts. It is useful to ascertain the kind of help offered, and the qualifications and experience of those involved in counselling.

*Registering
organizations*
British Association for Counselling
(BAC)
1 Regent Place
Rugby
Warwickshire CV21 2PJ
(office: 01788 550899)
(information line: 01788 578328)
(fax: 01788 562189)
(e-mail: bac@bac.co.uk)
BAC publishes lists of counselling
organizations and individual
counsellors in local areas. There
are information sheets available.

British Confederation of
Psychotherapists
37 Mapesbury Road
London NW2 4HJ
(0181 830 5173)
Produces a register of
psychoanalysts, analytic
psychologists, psychoanalytic
psychotherapists, child
psychotherapists.

The British Psychological Society
(BPS)
St Andrews House
48 Princess Road East
Leicester LE1 7DR
(0116 254 9568)
(fax: 0116 247 0787)
(e-mail: bps1@1e.ac.uk)
BPS keeps a register of chartered
clinical and counselling
psychologists.

United Kingdom Council for
Psychotherapy
167–9 Great Portland Street
London W1N 5FB
(0171 436 3002)
(fax: 0171 436 3013)
Produces a list of accredited
psychotherapists, by region.

United Kingdom Register of
Counsellors
1 Regent Place
Rugby
Warwickshire CV21 2PJ
(01788 550899)
(fax: 01788 546809)
Produces a list of accredited
counsellors.

*Organizations
offering training in,
or information
about, various forms
of counselling or
psychotherapy*
Association of Cognitive-Analytic
Therapists
CAT Training Secretary
Munro Clinic
Guy's Hospital
London SE1 9RT
(0171 955 2906)

British Association for Behavioural
and Cognitive Psychotherapies
c/o Rod Holland
Harrow Psychological Health
Services
Northwick Park Hospital
Watford Road
Harrow
Middlesex HA1 3UJ
(0181 869 2326)

British Association of
Psychotherapists
37 Mapesbury Road
London NW2 4HJ
(0181 452 9823)
(fax: 0181 452 5182)
Training and courses in
psychoanalytic psychotherapy,
analytic psychology, child
psychotherapy.

Centre for Multimodal Therapy and Centre for Rational Emotive Behaviour Therapy
156 Westcombe Hill
London SE3 7DH
(0181 293 4114)

Counselling in Primary Care Trust
Majestic House
High Street
Staines TW18 4DG
(01784 441782)
(fax: 01784 442601)

Institute of Transactional Analysis
Brian Leverson – Administrator
66 Paines Lane
Pinner
Middlesex HA5 3BL
(0181 8664288)
Produces a list of accredited TA therapists.

Psychosynthesis and Education Trust
92–4 Tooley Street
London SE1 2TH
(0171 403 2100)

Westminster Pastoral Foundation
23 Kensington Square
London W8 5HN
(0171 937 6956)
Offers counselling training.

Complementary therapies
Aromatherapy Organisations Council
3 Latymer Close
Braybrooke
Market Harborough
Leicester LE16 8LN
(01858 434242)
Massage using essential oils extracted from plants.

Association of Reflexologists
27 Old Gloucester Street
London WC1N 3XX
(0990 673320)
Massage of reflex points of the feet in order to release tension and imbalances in other parts of the body.

Bach Flower Remedies
Broadheath House
83 Parkside
Wimbledon
London SW19 5LP
(0181 780 4200)
Flower remedies used to balance emotional states and promote well-being. Useful 'rescue remedy' for panic states.

British Acupuncture Association and Register
22 Hockley Road
Rayleigh
Essex SS6 8EB
(01268 742534)
Acupuncture uses needles in the skin at specific points in order to regulate the energy flow in the body.

British Chiropractors' Association
5 First Avenue
Chelmsford
Essex CM1 1RX
(01245 353078)
Manipulation, especially of the spine, in order to restore pain-free function and movement.

General Council and Register of Naturopaths
Goswell House
2 Goswell Road
Somerset BA16 0JG
(01458 840072)
Naturopaths treat the whole person, looking thoroughly at the

way of life including diet, exercise and relaxation, and they use gentle manipulation techniques.

Institute for Complementary
Medicine
PO Box 194
London SE16 1QZ
(0171 237 5165)

The British Wheel of Yoga
1 Hamilton Place
Boston Road
Sleaford NG34 7ES
(01529 306851)
Gentle exercise involving stretching, breathing and meditation.

The General Council and Register of Osteopaths
56 London Street
Reading
Berkshire RG1 4SQ
(01734 576585)
Members have MRO after their names. Osteopathy uses rhythmic stretching, articulation and manipulation of various parts of the body in order to restore pain-free function and movement. It can help various disorders of the body by the effect of restoring spinal movement and promoting the free flow of energy throughout the body. Cranial osteopathy is a particularly gentle form of energy balancing used even on babies and small children.

The National Federation of Spiritual Healers
Old Manor Farm Studio
Church Street
Sunbury-on-Thames
Middlesex TW16 6RG
(01932 783164)
(fax: 01932 779648)

(referral service: 0891 616080 (9 a.m. to 5 p.m., Monday to Friday))
The NFSH runs training programmes and workshops. Spiritual healing is a gentle laying-on of hands, either touching the body or working on the aura around the body, and can help people physically, mentally, emotionally and spiritually. It is particularly useful for people who wish to experience deep relaxation but are afraid of touch.

The National Institute of Medical Herbalists
56 Longbrook Street
Exeter EX4 6AH
(01392 426022)
(fax: 01392 498963)
Herbal medicines used to treat most illnesses of the body and mind.

The UK Homeopathic Medical Association
6 Livingstone Road
Gravesend
Kent DA12 5DZ
(01474 560336)
Homeopathy treats the person with minute doses of substances that can stimulate the individual's own healing mechanism.

Agencies
Action for ME (Myalgic Encephalomeylitis)
PO Box 1302
Wells
Somerset BA5 1YE
(01749 670799)
(24-hour information line: 0891 122976)

Alcoholics Anonymous
PO Box 1
Stonebow House
Stonebow
York YO1 2NJ
(01904 644026)
(helpline: 0171 352 3001 (10 a.m.
to 10 p.m. every day))
Local helplines in local telephone
directory.

Al-Anon Family Groups UK and
Eire
61 Great Dover Street
London SE1 4YF
(0171 403 0888 (24-hour helpline))
Helps families and friends of
problem drinkers, whether the
alcoholic is still drinking or not.
Alateen, a part of Al-Anon, is for
young people aged 12 to 20 who
have been affected by someone
else's drinking, usually that of a
parent.

British Association of
Psychotherapists
37 Mapesbury Road
London NW2 4HJ
(0181 452 9823)
(fax: 0181 452 5182)
Can arrange for an initial
assessment for children,
adolescents and adults with
experienced therapists in
psychoanalytic and analytic
psychotherapy with subsequent
appropriate referral. GP's referral is
not necessary. Contacts in
Brighton, Bristol, Essex, Suffolk,
Oxford and York.

British Pregnancy Advisory Service
Austy Manor
Wootton Wawen
Solihull
West Midlands B95 6BX
(01564 793225)

Offers support and non-
judgemental counselling,
information and treatment for a
range of fertility-related problems.

Childline
2nd Floor
Royal Mail Building
Studd Street
London N1 0QW
(0171 239 1000)
(helpline: 0800 1111 (24-hours
every day))
(childline for children in care: 0800
884444 (6 p.m. to 10 p.m. daily))
Free national helplines offering
confidential counselling to children
in trouble or danger.

Childwatch
206 Hessle Road
Hull HU3 3BE
(answerphone: 01482 216681)
(fax: 01482 585214)
(helpline: 01482 325552 (10 a.m. to
10 p.m. Monday to Thursday))
Childwatch is an education and
prevention unit which refers cases
of abuse to the police and social
services. It also offers telephone
and face-to-face counselling for
adults who have been abused as
children.

Citizens Advice Bureaux
See entry under Citizens Advice
Bureaux in your local telephone
directory.

Cruse – Bereavement Care
Cruse House
126 Sheen Road
Richmond
Surrey TW9 1UR
(0181 940 4818 (general))
(helpline: 0181 332 7227 (9.30 a.m.
to 5 p.m., Monday to Friday))

Over 190 local branches offering counselling, practical advice and support. Publishes a wide range of literature.

Cry-sis
27 Old Gloucester Street
London WC1N 3XX
(0171 404 5011)
Cry-sis offers self-help and support for families with excessively crying, sleepless and demanding children.

Depression Alliance
35 Westminster Bridge Road
London SE1 7JB
(0171 633 0557)
For education, information and support.

Depressives Anonymous
36 Chestnut Avenue
Beverley
East Yorkshire HU17 9QU
(01482 860619)
Gives help and support. Pen-friend club.

Eating Disorders Association (EDA)
1st Floor
Wensum House
103 Prince of Wales Road
Norwich
Norfork NR1 1DW
(01603 619090 (information, 9 a.m. to 5 p.m.))
(adults: 01603 621414 (helpline, 9 a.m. to 6.30 p.m., Monday to Friday, and answerphone))
(youthline: 01603 765050 (4 p.m. to 6 p.m., Monday to Friday)
Supports and advises sufferers of anorexia and bulimia nervosa, also their families and friends. Network of self-help groups.

Gamblers Anonymous
PO Box 88
London SW10 0EU
(0171 384 3040 (24-hour helpline))
A self-help group of men and women who share a problem with gambling. Details of local meetings.

Home-Start UK
2 Salisbury Road
Leicester LE1 7QR
(0116 233 9955)
Can advise on local Home-Start schemes giving advice, support and friendship to families with children under five.

Institute of Family Therapy
24–32 Stephenson Way
London NW1 2HX
(0171 391 9150)
Provides couple and family therapy and a mediation service. Also counsels bereaved families and those with someone in their family who is seriously ill. (Donations welcome.) Self-referral possible.

Institute of Psychosexual Medicine
11 Chandos Street
Off Cavendish Square
London W1M 9DE
(0171 580 0631)
Has a list of NHS and private doctors trained in psychosexual counselling. Send a SAE for its list.

International Stress Management Association
David Moore
Division of Psychology
South Bank University
103 Borough Road
London SE1 0AA
(07000 780430)

(fax: 01992 426673)
(e-mail: stress@isma.org.uk)
Can give information and advice on the best ways to tackle stress, particularly if it is work-related.

Kidscape
152 Buckingham Palace Road
London SW1W 9TR
(0171 730 3300)
Campaigns for children's safety, does programmes in schools and has useful literature for both children and parents to read.

Lesbian and Gay Bereavement Project
Colindale Hospital
London NW9 5HG
(0181 455 8894)
Gives name of volunteer and phone number for each day. Helpline for gays and lesbians who have lost a partner through death. Also offers practical help on funeral arrangements, inquests and wills.

London Lesbian and Gay Switchboard
PO Box 7324
London N1 9QS
(office: 0171 837 6768)
(fax: 0171 837 7300)
(helpline: 0171 837 7324 (24-hour))
Information service to lesbians and gay men.

London Rape Crisis Centre
PO Box 69
London WC1X 9NJ
(0171 916 5466)
(helpline: 0171 837 1600 (weekdays 6 p.m. to 10 p.m., weekends 10 a.m. to 10 p.m.))
Counsels victims of rape or sexual violence either personally or through its helpline.

Manic Depression Fellowship
8–10 High Street
Kingston-upon-Thames
Surrey KT1 1EY
(0181 974 6550)
Helps sufferers of manic depression and their relatives via a network of local groups.

ME Association (Myalgic Encephalomyelitis)
4 Corringham Road
Stanford-Le-Hope
Essex SS17 0AH
(counselling service and office: 01375 642466)
(advice line: 01375 361013 (1.30 p.m. to 4 p.m. Monday to Friday))
(fax: 01375 360256)
Provides advice and support to people with ME.

MIND (National Association for Mental Health)
Granta House
15–19 Broadway
Stratford
London E15 4BQ
(general office line: 0181 519 2122 (also contact number for legal advice Monday, Wednesday, Friday, 2 p.m. to 4.30 p.m.))
(information line: 0181 522 1728 (10 a.m. to 12.30 p.m. and 4.30 p.m., Monday to Friday))
MIND has over 240 local associations, and local groups offer a range of activities including counselling, drop-in centres, relatives' support schemes, employment projects and befriending schemes. MIND offer a series of information leaflets on a range of mental health conditions and issues.

National Childbirth Trust
Alexandra House
Oldham Terrace
London W3 6NH
(0181 992 8637 (9.30 a.m. to 4.30
p.m., Monday to Friday))
Offers information and support in
pregnancy, childbirth and early
parenthood. Three hundred and
eighty local groups provide various
services such as natural childbirth
classes, help with breast-feeding,
post-natal support, miscarriage and
bereavement support.

National Retreat Association
Central Hall
256 Bermondsey Street
London SE1 3UJ
(0171 357 7736 (9 a.m. to 5 p.m.))
(fax: 0171 357 7724)

National Schizophrenia Fellowship
(NSF)
28 Castle Street
Kingston-upon-Thames
Surrey KT1 1SS
(general inquiries: 0181 547 3937)
(advice: 0181 974 6814)
NSF gives support, information,
advice and advocacy to
schizophrenic sufferers and their
families and emphasizes support
and respite for relatives. NSF runs
support groups for carers and
Voices, a group for people with
schizophrenia.

NSPCC (National Society for the
Prevention of Cruelty to Children)
42 Curtain Road
London EC2A 3NH
(0171 825 2500)
(0800 800500 (freefone 24-hour
helpline))
For the protection and support of
abused children and their families.

Overeaters Anonymous (OA)
PO Box 19
Stretford
Manchester M32 9EB
(0161 762 9348 (gives details on
answerphone of all local numbers
and different areas where the
groups run))
Gives information and support to
people with weight problems via
group meetings throughout the
UK.

Parents Anonymous
8 Manor Gardens
London N7 6LA
(0171 263 8918 (answerphone with
details of volunteer for that day))
Crisis support and counselling for
parents of children who are
critically ill in hospital and for
parents and family who have lost a
child through sudden death.

POPAN (Prevention of Professional
Abuse Network)
1 Wyvil Court
Wyvil Road
London SW8 2TG
(0171 622 6334)
(fax: 0171 622 9788)

Quit (Smoking)
Victoria House
70 Tottenham Court Road
London W1P 0HA
office: 0171 388 5775
(helpline: 0171 487 3000 (1 p.m. to
9 p.m., Monday to Friday; 1 p.m.
to 5 p.m., weekends; answerphone
outside these hours))
Advice and counselling and
information about local support
groups.

Relate
Herbert Gray College
Little Church Street

Rugby
Warwickshire CV21 3AP
(0178 857 3241)
Offers counselling to people with
relationship problems. Sexual
therapy and a family mediation
service are also available.

Release
388 Old Street
London EC1V 9LT
(adviceline: 0171 729 9904 (10 a.m.
to 6 p.m., Monday to Friday)
(helpline: 0171 603 8654 (24-
hour))
Offers advice, information and
referral on legal and drug-related
problems for users, families and
friends.

Samaritans
10 The Grove
Slough
Berkshire SL1 1PQ
(information and enquiries: 01753
532713)
(national helpline: 0345 909090
(local call rate))
(Internet: Jo@Samaritans.org or
Samaritans@anonpenct.fi)
The Samaritans provides
confidential support to suicidal and
despairing people, 24 hours every
day.

SANE (Schizophrenia a National
Emergency)
199–205 Old Marylebone Road
London NW1 5QP
(0171 724 6520)
(Saneline: 0345 67 8000 (2 p.m. to
12 midnight, calls charged at local
rate))
SANE is a national charity aiming
to increase funding of research into
causes and possible cures of
serious mental illness. There is a

legal department. Saneline gives
information about resources.

Seasonal Affective Disorder
Association (SADA)
PO Box 989
Steyning DN44 3HG
(0181 969 7028)
Seasonal Affective Disorder (SAD)
is a regularly recurring winter
depression. SADA is a self-help
organization giving advice and
support.

Tavistock Clinic
120 Belsize Lane
London NW3 5BA
(0171 435 7111)
Offers short-term and long-term
individual psychotherapy and
group therapy. Referrals must be
made by a GP or other
professional. Adult, adolescent,
child and family departments.

Terrence Higgins Trust
52–4 Gray's Inn Road
London WC1X 8JU
(0171 831 0330)
(helpline: 0171 242 1010 (12 noon
to 10 p.m., daily))
(legal line: 0171 405 2381 (7 p.m.
to 9 p.m., Monday and
Wednesday)
Telephone counselling to people
who are HIV positive or have
AIDS, and their families. Advice
and information and support
services (such as the Buddy
Scheme which offers befriending
to people living with AIDS).

Ticehurst House Hospital
Ticehurst
Wadhurst
Sussex TN5 7HU
(01580 200391)

This hospital sees people suffering from post-traumatic stress, eating disorders, drug and alcohol abuse.

Turning Point
New Loom House
101 Back Church Lane
London E1 1LU
(0171 702 2300)
Over 45 projects offering residential rehabilitation, day care and street level advice to people with drink, drug and mental health problems.

Westminster Pastoral Foundation (WPF)
23 Kensington Square
London W8 5HN
(0171 937 6956)
Centres in London and throughout UK offering a range of counselling services including individual, couple, family and group therapy.

Women's Aid Federation
PO Box 391
Bristol BS99 7WS
(office: 0117 944 4411)
(fax: 0117 924 1703)
(helpline: 0345 023468)
Local groups offering counselling, practical help and a refuge for women and children who are suffering emotional, mental or physical violence, harassment or sexual abuse.

Women's Therapy Centre
10 Manor Gardens
London N7 6JS
(0171 263 6200)
Information and education. Special expertise in all the eating disorders. Psychotherapy offered (London).

Appendix 1

Questionnaire Administered to Practising and Training Counsellors, with Analysis

Referral and termination issues questionnaire

I am very grateful to you for your help. If you wish any of your referral or termination experiences to be included in the book, either named or anonymously, please detail on a separate sheet.

1   Do you formally assess each new client?
    Yes/No

2   Do you work privately/medical setting/for an organization?

3   How would you describe your theoretical orientation?

4   Do you refer clients to other professionals?
    Often/Sometimes/Never

5   To which professionals have you/would you be most likely to refer?
    (Other counsellor/psychotherapist, general practitioner, psychiatrist, psychologist, complementary therapist)

6 If you never or rarely refer clients elsewhere please describe your reasons.

7 Are there any particular client problems that you prefer not to deal with?

8 Have you ever kept on working with a client who, with hindsight, it might have been better to refer elsewhere?

9 Do you maintain an up-to-date file of professionals' details in case you need to make a referral?

10 Have you experienced particular difficulties in making a needed referral?
(Please describe.)

11 Do you contract a set number of sessions in advance with a client?

12 Who decides when the counselling terminates?
Client/Counsellor/Joint decision

13 Do you believe that clients should always work through termination?
Yes/No
If yes, how long does this take?

14 Do you offer an 'open door' for future counselling sessions?

15 Have any of your clients terminated abruptly?
Often/Sometimes/Never
Did you follow this up? (Phone, letter)

16 What feelings do you experience if a client terminates abruptly?

17 Have you ever experienced difficulty terminating with a client?
(Client did not wish to end; you did not wish to end.)

18 Have you ever made friends with a former client?

Analysis of responses

This questionnaire was administered to forty counsellors in practice and twenty trainee counsellors. The following analysis is taken from the forty counsellors in practice. The responses of the trainee counsellors to Questions 6, 9, 16 and 18 were particularly noted. (Question 6 asked for reasons if the counsellor never referred, Question 9 asked about up-to-date professionals' details for referral purposes, Question 16 asked about feelings of the counsellor when a client terminates abruptly, and Question 18 asked whether the counsellor had ever made friends with a former client.) The number of counsellors who answered the questionnaire represents a small percentage of all practising counsellors and so the responses can only indicate possibilities or tendencies amongst counsellors.

Question 1
- 60% of counsellors said that they formally assess each new client.
- All of the counsellors who indicated that they formally assess each new client work at least part-time in a medical setting or for an organization.
- All of the counsellors who only work privately indicated that they do not use formal assessment procedures.

Question 2
- 10% of counsellors work only privately.
- 0% work only in a medical setting.
- 10% work only for an organization.
- 10% work privately and in a medical setting.
- 50% work privately and for an organization.
- 0% work in a medical setting and for an organization.
- 20% work in all three categories.

Question 3
- 30% of counsellors described their orientation as eclectic.
- 10% described their orientation as person-centred.
- 10% described their orientation as humanistic/eclectic.
- 10% described their orientation as transpersonal.
- 20% described their orientation as psychodynamic.
- 20% described their orientation as integrative.

Question 4
All counsellors reported referring clients to other professionals.

Question 5
Counsellors referred clients to counsellors or psychotherapist (60%), general practitioner (50%), psychiatrist (30%), psychologist (50%), complementary therapist (30%).

Question 6
Some trainee counsellors assumed that if they were working in a GP practice that all the referrals would be suitable and hence there was no need to refer the client elsewhere.

Question 7
Individual counsellors indicated one or more of the following areas that they would prefer not to deal with: eating disorders, child abuse, sexual abuse, abusers, psychiatric patients, psychotic patients, personality disorder, psychopathic behaviour, alcohol abuse, drug abuse, psychosexual problems, couples.

Question 8
80% of counsellors answered in the affirmative – that with hindsight it would have been better to have referred a particular client.

Question 9
60% of the counsellors kept an up-to-date file of referral details. For the trainee counsellors the response to this question depended on the requirement of the training course.

Question 10
Some counsellors mentioned long waiting lists especially for psychologists and community mental health teams or unavailability for specialities such as post-traumatic stress disorder or eating disorders.

Question 11
50% of counsellors contract a set number of sessions with a client but half of these counsellors would negotiate an extension.

Question 12
- 10% of counsellors marked only that the clients decided to terminate the counselling.
- 40% marked only joint decision.
- 20% marked client decision and joint decision.
- 30% marked all three choices.

Question 13
- 70% of counsellors believe that clients should always work through termination, or 'if possible'. This could take from one to ten sessions or 'variable'.
- 30% of counsellors did not believe that clients should always work through termination.

Question 14
- 80% of counsellors said that they would offer an 'open door' for future counselling sessions.
- 20% of counsellors said that they would not offer an 'open door' for future counselling sessions.

Question 15
- 90% of counsellors indicated that clients sometimes terminated abruptly. This was followed up by 70% of counsellors.
- 10% of counsellors phoned the client, 40% of counsellors wrote, 20% used the phone and letter.

Question 16

The following feelings were reported by counsellors if a client terminates abruptly: concern, regret, disappointment, sadness, surprise, confusion, shock, anxiety, annoyance, anger, guilt, relief, pleasure. There could be a sense of puzzlement, dissatisfaction, failure, inadequacy, rejection, things being unfinished or left hanging. Some counsellors reported acceptance and feelings of success. There might be a questioning whether the abrupt termination was due to the client or the counsellor. Trainee counsellors felt particularly vulnerable and tended to question their competence.

Question 17

- 90% of counsellors had experienced difficulty terminating with a client.
- 40% indicated that this was because the client did not wish to end.
- 10% indicated that this was because the counsellor did not wish to end.

Question 18

- 80% of counsellors did not make friends with former clients. One counsellor stated, 'It doesn't work!'
- 20% of counsellors indicated that they had made friends with a former client.
- The same percentages apply to the trainee counsellors.

Appendix 2

Sample Letter to GP

12 West Road,
Rainham,
Kent ME7 6PF.

Rainham Health Centre,
Sycamore Street,
Rainham,
Kent ME7 2TK.   30th January 1998

Dear Dr Patel,

Re: Susan Kinwood (d.o.b. 24.3.58), 16 Treetop Avenue, Rainham, Kent.

I have been seeing Susan for private counselling for the last three months in order that she could explore her general unhappiness and anxieties. Although Susan's mood has lifted and she is better able to deal with her anxiety, we have uncovered a specific phobia about spiders which appears to be deeply seated. Susan is keen to overcome this fear and she will be coming to see you in the near future with the hope that you will be able to arrange some specialist psychological help for her.

Yours sincerely,

Mary Dartmore, Dip. Couns.,
BAC Accredited Counsellor.

Appendix 3

Example of Formal Assessment Form

Date
Referred by
Name
Occupation
Date of birth
Address

Tel. (home)
Tel. (work)
GP
GP's address

GP's tel.

Client Assessment

Childhood history

Past significant events

Significant relationships

Work

Support network

Specific problem areas

Medication and hospitalization

Personal strengths

Other relevant details

Contraindications for counselling/indications for referral

Goals

Plan of action

References

Assagioli, R. (1965) *Psychosynthesis: A Manual of Principles and Techniques*. Wellingborough: Thorson.

Aveline, M. (1993) 'The training and supervision of individual therapists', in W. Dryden (ed.), *Individual Therapy: A Handbook*. Milton Keynes: Open University Press.

BAC (1996a) *Code of Ethics and Practice for Counsellors*. Rugby: British Association for Counselling.

BAC (1996b) *Code of Ethics and Practice for Supervisors of Counsellors*. Rugby: British Association for Counselling.

BAC (1997) *Code of Ethics and Practice for Trainers*. Rugby: British Association for Counselling.

Barkham, M. (1989) 'Brief prescriptive therapy in two-plus-one sessions: initial cases from the clinic', *Behavioural Psychotherapy*, 17: 161–75.

Bloch, S. (1979) 'Assessment of patients for psychotherapy', *British Journal of Psychiatry*, 135: 193–208.

Bond, T. (1993) *Standards and Ethics for Counselling in Action*. London: Sage.

Bornstein, R.F. (1993) 'Dependency and patienthood', *Journal of Clinical Psychology*, 49 (3): 397–405.

Boscolo, L. and Bertrando, P. (1993) *The Times of Time: A New Perspective in Systematic Therapy and Consultation*. New York: Norton.

British National Formulary (1996) London: British Medical Association and Royal Pharmaceutical Society of Great Britain.

Corey, M.S. and Corey, G. (1989) *Becoming a Helper*. Pacific Grove, CA: Brooks/Cole.

Culley, S. (1991) *Integrative Counselling Skills in Action*. London: Sage.

Cummings, N. and Sayana, M. (1995) *Focused Psychotherapy: A Casebook of Brief, Intermittent Psychotherapy throughout the Life Cycle*. New York: Brunner/Mazel.

Daines, B., Gask, L. and Usherwood, T. (1997) *Medical and Psychiatric Issues for Counsellors*. London: Sage.

Davies, D. and Neal, C. (eds) (1996) *Pink Therapy: A Guide for Counsellors and Therapists working with Lesbian, Gay and Bisexual Clients*. Buckingham: Open University Press.

Delvey, J., Jr (1985) 'Beyond the blank screen: the patient's search for an emotional container in the therapist', *Psychotherapy*, 22 (3): 583–6.

Drew, T. and King, M. (1995) *The Mental Health Handbook*. London: Piatkus.

Dryden, W. (ed.) (1989) *Key Issues for Counselling in Action*. London: Sage.

Dryden, W. (1990) *Rational-Emotive Counselling in Action*. London: Sage.

Dryden, W. (ed.) (1993) *Questions and Answers on Counselling in Action*. London: Sage.

Dryden, W. (ed.) (1996) *Handbook of Individual Therapy*. London: Sage.

Dryden, W. and Feltham, C. (1992) *Brief Counselling: A Practical Guide for Beginning Practitioners*. Buckingham: Open University Press.

Dryden, W. and Feltham, C. (1994) *Developing the Practice of Counselling*. London: Sage.

Dryden, W. and Feltham, C. (1995) *Counselling and Psychotherapy: A Consumer's Guide*. London: Sheldon Press.

Egan, G. (1994) *The Skilled Helper: A Problem-Management Approach to Helping*, 5th edn. Pacific Grove, CA: Brooks/Cole.

Erdman, P. (1994) 'Supervisor development: how it affects supervisees', *Counselling*, 5 (4): 275–9.

Evans, H. (1996) *Help! How and Where to Find the Answer to your Every Problem*. London: Macmillan.

Feltham, C. (1997) *Time-Limited Counselling*. London: Sage.

Fontana, D. (1989) *Managing Stress*. Leicester: BPS/Routledge.

Freud, S. (1937) *Analysis Terminable and Interminable*. Standard Edition, 23: 216–53. London: Hogarth Press, 1964.

Garfield, S.L. (1982) 'Eclecticism and integrationism in psychotherapy', *Behaviour Therapy*, 13: 610–23.

Garfield, S.L. (1989) *The Practice of Brief Psychotherapy*. New York: Pergamon.

Gelder, M., Gath, D. and Mayou, R. (1989) *Oxford Textbook of Psychiatry*. Oxford: Oxford University Press.

Grollman, E.A. (1987) *Living When a Loved One Has Died*. Boston: Beacon Press.

Halgin, R.P. and Caron, M. (1991) 'To treat or not to treat: considerations for referring prospective clients', *Psychotherapy in Private Practice*, 8 (4): 87–95.

Howard, K.I., Kopta, S.M., Krause, M.S. and Orlinsky, D.E. (1986) 'The dose–response relationship in psychotherapy', *American Psychologist*, 41: 159–64.

Hutchins, D.E. (1989) 'Improving the counseling relationship', in W. Dryden (ed.), *Key Issues for Counselling in Action*. London: Sage.

Inskipp, F. and Proctor, B. (1993) *The Art, Craft and Tasks of Counselling Supervision, Part 1: Making the Most of Supervision – Professional Development for Counsellors, Psychotherapists, Supervisors and Trainees*. Twickenham: Cascade.

Jenkins, P. (1997) *Counselling, Psychotherapy and the Law*. London: Sage.

Kottler, J.A. (1990) *On Being a Therapist*. Oxford: Jossey-Bass.

Kupers, T.A. (1988) *Ending Therapy*. New York: New York University Press.

Lago, C. and Thompson, J. (1989) 'Counselling and race', in W. Dryden, D. Charles-Edwards and R. Woolfe (eds), *Handbook of Counselling in Britain*. London: Routledge.

Lakin, M. (1988) *Ethical Issues in the Psychotherapies*. Oxford: Oxford University Press.

Lamb, D.H. (1985) 'A time-frame model of termination in psychotherapy', *Psychotherapy*, 22 (3): 605–9.

Lazarus, A.A. (1989) *The Practice of Multimodal Therapy: Systematic, Comprehensive, and Effective Psychotherapy*. Baltimore, MD: Johns Hopkins University Press.

Leitman, N. (1995) 'To the point', *Counselling News*, 20: 3.

Maholick, L.T. and Turner, D.W. (1979) 'Termination: that difficult farewell', *American Journal of Psychotherapy*, 33: 583–91.

Mahrer, A.R. (1988) 'The briefest psychotherapy', *Changes*, 6 (3): 86–9.

Malan, D.H. (1979) *Individual Psychotherapy and the Science of Psychodynamics*. Cambridge: Butterworths.

Masson, J. (1990) *Against Therapy*. London: Fontana.

Mearns, D. (1993) 'The ending phase of counselling', in W. Dryden (ed.), *Questions and Answers on Counselling in Action*. London: Sage.

Mearns, D. and Thorne, B. (1988) *Person-Centred Counselling in Action*. London: Sage.

Orlinsky, D.E. and Howard, K.I. (1986) 'Process and outcome in psychotherapy', in S.L. Garfield and A.E. Bergin (eds), *Handbook of Psychotherapy and Behaviour Change*, 3rd edn. Chichester: Wiley.

Palmer, S. and Dryden, W. (1995) *Counselling for Stress Problems*. London: Sage.

Palmer, S. and McMahon, G. (eds) (1997) *Client Assessment*. London: Sage.

Peck, M. Scott (1990) *People of the Lie: The Hope for Healing Human Evil*. London: Arrow.

Pipes, R.B., Schwartz, R. and Crouch, P. (1985) 'Measuring client fears', *Journal of Consulting and Clinical Psychology*, 53 (6): 933–4.

Ramsey, G.V. (1962) 'The referral task in counselling', *Personnel and Guidance Journal*, January: 443–7.

Rogers, C.R. (1951) *Client-Centred Therapy*. London: Constable.

Rogers, C.R. (1989) *On Becoming a Person: A Therapist's View of Psychotherapy*. London: Constable.

Rosenfield, M. (1997) *Counselling by Telephone*. London: Sage.

Rowan, J. (1993) *The Transpersonal: Psychotherapy and Counselling*. London: Routledge.

Rowan, J. and Dryden, W. (eds) (1988) *Innovative Therapy in Britain*. Milton Keynes: Open University Press.

Rowe, D. (1991) *Breaking the Bonds: Understanding Depression, Finding Freedom*. London: Fontana.

Russell, J. (1993) *Out of Bounds: Sexual Exploitation in Counselling and Therapy*. London: Sage.

Rutter, P. (1991) *Sex in the Forbidden Zone*. London: HarperCollins.

Ryle, A. (1991) *Cognitive-Analytic Therapy: Active Participation in Change – A New Integration in Brief Psychotherapy*. Chichester: Wiley.

Shapiro, R.J. (1974) 'Therapist attitudes and premature termination in family and individual therapy', *Journal of Nervous and Mental Disease*, 159 (2): 101–7.

Shipton, G. and Smith, E. (1998) *Long-Term Counselling*. London: Sage.

Siebold, C. (1991) 'Termination: when the therapist leaves', *Clinical Social Work Journal*, 19 (2): 191–204.

Sills, C. (ed.) (1997) *Contracts in Counselling*. London: Sage.

Skynner, A.C.R. (1969) 'A group-analytic approach to conjoint family therapy', *Journal of Child Psychology and Psychiatry*, 10: 81–106.

Skynner, A.C.R. and Brown, D.G. (1981) 'Referral of patients for psychotherapy', *British Medical Journal*, 282: 1952–5.

Smith, M.L., Glass, G.V. and Miller, T.I. (1980) *The Benefits of Psychotherapy*. Baltimore, MD: Johns Hopkins University Press.

Stout, C. (1993) *From the Other Side of the Couch: Candid Conversations with Psychiatrists and Psychologists*. Westport, CT: Greenwood Press.

Sutherland, N.S. (1987) *Breakdown: A Personal Crisis and a Medical Dilemma*, 2nd edn. London: Weidenfeld & Nicolson.

Sutton, C. (1989) 'The evaluation of counselling: a goal-attainment approach', in W. Dryden (ed.), *Key Issues for Counselling in Action*. London: Sage.

Szasz, T. (1986) 'The case against suicide prevention', *American Psychologist*, 41: 806–12.

Talmon, M. (1990) *Single Session Therapy: Maximizing the Effect of the First (and Often Only) Therapeutic Encounter*. San Francisco, CA: Jossey-Bass.

Trayner, B. and Clarkson, C. (1992) 'What happens if a psychotherapist dies?', *Counselling*, 3 (1): 23–4.

Van Bilsen, H.P.J.G. (1996) *Treating Addictive Behaviours: A Manual of Brief Therapy for Addictions*. Chichester: Wiley.

Walker, M. (1993) 'When values clash', in W. Dryden (ed.), *Questions and Answers on Counselling in Action*. London: Sage.

Ward, D.E. (1984) 'Termination of individual counseling: concepts and strategies', *Journal of Counseling and Development*, 63: 21–5.

Watkins, C.E., Jr (1983) 'Counselor acting out in the counseling situation: an exploratory analysis', *Personnel and Guidance Journal*, 61: 417–23.

Watkins, C.E., Jr (1989) 'Countertransference: its impact on the counseling situation', in W. Dryden (ed.), *Key Issues for Counselling in Action*. London: Sage.

Williams, S. (1993) *An Incomplete Guide to Referral Issues for Counsellors*. Manchester: PCCS Books.

Wilson, J.E. (1996) *Time-Conscious Psychological Therapy: A Life Stage to Go Through*. London: Routledge.

Wise, M.J. and Rinn, R.C. (1983) 'Premature client termination from psychotherapy as a function of continuity of care', *Journal of Psychiatric Treatment and Evaluation*, 5: 63–5.

Wood, E.C. and Wood, C.D. (1990) 'Referral issues in psychotherapy and psychoanalysis', *American Journal of Psychotherapy*, XLIV (1): 85–94.

Worden, J.W. (1991) *Grief Counselling and Grief Therapy*. London: Routledge.

Zeig, J.K. and Gilligan, S.G. (eds) (1990) *Brief Therapy: Myths, Methods and Metaphors*. New York: Brunner/Mazel.

Index